A Handbook *for* Steiner-Waldorf Class Teachers

Also published in partnership with
the Steiner Waldorf Schools Fellowship:

The Care and Development of the Human Senses
by Willi Aeppli

Language Teaching in Steiner-Waldorf Schools
by Johannes Kiersch

Religious Education in Steiner-Waldorf Schools
edited by Helmut Kügelgen and Tilde von Eiff

Report Verses in Rudolf Steiner's Art of Education
by Heinz Müller

Rudolf Steiner's Curriculum for Steiner-Waldorf Schools
by E. A. Karl Stockmeyer

The Tasks and Content of the Steiner-Waldorf Curriculum
edited by Martyn Rawson and Kevin Avison

Towards Creative Teaching
edited by Martyn Rawson and Kevin Avison

www.florisbooks.co.uk

A Handbook *for* Steiner-Waldorf Class Teachers

Compiled and written by
KEVIN AVISON

Floris Books

First published in 1995 by Steiner Waldorf Schools Fellowship

This third, revised edition published in 2016 by Floris Books
in association with the Steiner Waldorf Schools Fellowship

Third printing 2022

British Library CIP Data available
ISBN 978-178250-249-4
Printed in Great Britain by Bell & Bain Ltd

Floris Books supports sustainable forest management by
printing this book on materials made from wood that
comes from responsible sources and reclaimed material

MIX
Paper from
responsible sources
FSC
www.fsc.org   FSC® C007785

Contents

Dedication

This book is dedicated to hardworking teachers (Waldorf and otherwise) everywhere, without whose kleptomania this collection of propositions and prompts would not exist.

The handbook owes its existence to the work of those teachers. Some of the ideas detailed within have been caught while I have been sitting in your classrooms as an adviser, attending conferences or workshops, or hearing your thoughts in professional and informal discussion. Any ideas I could claim as my own have arisen through that dialogue.

I have found that where there is conversation, engagement and serious interest in improvement, new practical initiatives develop. A teacher needs to be a collector of cultural artefacts, an intellectual magpie; fresh ideas arise and grow from creative theft. Nonetheless, the handbook is my responsibility and its shortcomings and errors are mine and mine alone.

Introduction

Readers of the previous version of this handbook will find the new version substantially changed. Apologies to anyone who now feels they are forced to replace their 2004 edition; I hope you will find the new one worth the cost.

We live in a time of rapid and uncertain change with little that can be taken for granted. The world in this quarter of the early twenty-first century is one of increasing complication, as institutions of every type buckle under stress or decay. Cultural agents and organisations that support them are under continual, and often hostile, scrutiny. The Confucian saying, 'Without trust we cannot stand', seems far from our current preoccupations or public habits. Yet without mutual confidence and self-belief there can be no improvement, and this applies to schools and school staff as much as it does to other types of organisation.

My work for the Steiner Waldorf Schools Fellowship as advisory co-ordinator has enabled me to observe both proficient teachers and those struggling to develop their craft. My fellow advisers regularly share stories of educational valour, and I am immensely grateful to all the colleagues who, by opening their classroom doors, have created opportunities for instigating professional dialogue. Those of us who have been privileged to visit a range of classes are aware that we have a deep responsibility to communicate these ideas. I hope this volume can be understood as an attempt to fulfil a part of that responsibility.

Most importantly, the innovation of providing the handbook with a web resource to enable readers to access worksheets, pro formas and other copyable material has enabled a more holistic presentation, with the aim of giving those who have requested it a series of footholds on the frequently treacherous path the teacher has to tread. (These are available at www.florisbooks.co.uk/books/Steiner-Waldorf-Handbook)

Please note that while this is a reprint of the 2016 handbook, there has been one change in the removal of Appendix X from the book. Although I have yet to meet any colleague who failed to understand that short section as humorous caricature, warning of the danger of teachers over-personalising their relationship with the class, the piece sadly became victim to misrepresentation in the media and so has been removed.

Remember, this is not an 'official' handbook. Everything here is provisional and intended to give you, the reader, ideas, suggestions or provocations for your own work. Nothing included in this book has any standing or status other than the value you place on it through finding it useful.

Let me know what you find useful and please continue to share your thoughts. When I am able to do so, I will always acknowledge the source of these shared ideas. Colleagues are invited to steal back whatever advances the learning process (you are entirely justified in doing so), adapting these things according to need, circumstance and disposition. In that way it is my hope that we can continue to improve what we offer to children and young people.

Part I
Practical Considerations

1.

The imponderables

This handbook is mainly concerned with 'basic skills'. These are the capabilities that children need to become effective adults and ensure they are able to give their lives purpose and direction. As Waldorf educators we seek to provide what children need to develop a meaningful and practical relationship with the world, one that enables them to grow in understanding, empathy and positive self-direction, and to become life-long learners.

Basic skills are the medium through which so many relationships spring to life and are also the way a person interacts with others within shared cultures. But to concentrate exclusively upon such skills would diminish real education. This is where what Rudolf Steiner called 'the imponderables' of the teacher's art make their entrance, and it is here that the creativity of the teacher begins to work. But nonetheless, the ebb of creative teaching needs to work in conjunction with the disciplined flow of basic skills.

It may be that so little attention is paid to developing these fundamentals that we fail to bring them into focus. So many educational initiatives and policies seem to involve hacking through the subtler aspects of learning that there is a danger of failing to see what is good and positive for young people in the work of teachers outside the Waldorf movement. We can learn from the way Rudolf Steiner spoke about biodynamic agriculture: adopting sound practices in food production and infusing it with what comes from spiritual science because the two complement one another. The same practice applies to placing basic skills to the forefront of this handbook; deeper questions will always be present in the background.

There are many lectures and resources that address the need for a teacher to develop their reflective practice and thus their capacity to reach children throughout their career. A sound grasp of basic skills and knowledge of when children have reached each stage of a class should inspire confidence to create, innovate and produce a self-assurance grounded in practical idealism.

Education is a process, one in which the continuing development of the teacher is a vital ingredient. Through this continued practice of improvement, teaching and learning are brought into a virtuous circle, mutually reinforcing one another. The late Wim Moleman of the Netherlands Advisory Institute, one of my mentors, once said when speaking on organisational consultancy, 'However much you know, you'll mostly get things wrong. You then learn to put it right!'.

Rudolf Steiner describes it in what may seem like more direct terms:

If we say to ourselves, 'At the beginning of the school year, I had excellent educational principles, I have followed the best educational authorities, have done everything to carry out these principles' – if you really had done this, you really would have taught badly. You would certainly have taught best if each morning you had gone into your class in fear and trembling without much confidence in yourself and then had said at the end of the year: 'You yourself have really learned most during this year'.

September 15, 1920,
Inner Attitudes of the Teacher

'Fear and trembling' may not seem conducive to teaching or self-education; however, a mood of humility provides a sound basis for both. Teaching is, after all, an 'awesome' profession (if we reinstate the epithet to its original meaning, i.e. to inspire 'awe'). Awe, and a wonderful curiosity of the vast ocean of all there is to be learned, coupled with the resolution to do everything better, may seem like a daunting concept, but it is also what defines a learner. There is no better way to refute the addiction most governments have to policies that aim to 'standardise teaching, control through testing and make failure impossible'. This is a recipe for the kind of mediocrity that the official view of things prefers to call 'outstanding'.

We also need to apply Steiner's scepticism about 'excellent principles' to Waldorf practices and precepts. The curriculum exists for the children, not the children for the curriculum. Rudolf Steiner clearly intended that his indications would be starting points, not a destination in themselves. The teacher needs a place from which to begin their quest to become an educator, or to put it another way:

…out of mere emptiness nothing can be made, but the imperfect can be perfected. Anyone who develops the propensity for creative activity is capable of dealing with all that life brings in the best way.

The curriculum of the first Waldorf School is a rich source of these starting points, along with subsequent work done by former and contemporary colleagues. That brings us to what newer colleagues sometimes refer to as…

'The anthroposophy thing'

I have sometimes had this put to me as a semi-question: 'I'm not really sure about the anthroposophy thing'. Often it appears that the inquirer is looking for a single or simple set of answers to the question, 'What has anthroposophy to do with my teaching?'. I think the question easily becomes misleading because it suggests an underlying relationship between anthroposophy and teaching in a Waldorf school that is topsy-turvy.

First, let's be clear, what we're concerned about here is not the whole of anthroposophy, but the principles and practice of Waldorf education and especially the values of education.[1] But, in the matter of teacher education and self-education (and the latter is crucial), the essentials are a matter of process, a matter of doing. Waldorf education is not about belief, but of heartfelt certainty discovered through the activity of teaching and including active thinking and honest reflection.

Any process will have an implicit logic embedded within it and that logic can be thought, felt and lived. Without a sense for this, practice can degenerate into ritual or dogma. These are ever-present dangers found when breaking the surface from total immersion in an unexamined normality. For 'normal' is what we call the unchallenged collective of a filtered and pre-constituted life. The logic of Waldorf education rises out of normality to provide clear-sightedness for what lies behind the scenes. Doing this is a process that involves what Owen Barfield called 'participative thinking'. [2]

The logic of Waldorf may be first encountered in a number of ways: through doing and experiencing, through feeling its meaningfulness, or through perceiving it directly in one's own thinking. Most often, recognition of Waldorf logic starts with a glimpse: 'I see this makes complete sense for the children'. That first moment of recognition then needs to be checked in practice, then tested and observed through deep reflection. Restricting critical enquiry tends to lead to ritual and is likely to be ousted by more compelling, if often temporary, fads and attachments.

Commitment to practice and patience is as necessary to becoming a Waldorf teacher as it is to defining the difference between infatuation and a long-term relationship. Every teacher has to fulfil the necessary professional requirements of teaching: legal, regulatory, and ethical. Waldorf teachers have a double commitment: first to those defined requirements (the essential training in policy and procedure, the 'bureaucratic stuff' that is set in place to ensure we are taking proper care of the children); but also, alongside that, to the commitment that is needed for developing a professional practice through meditative attention and self-critical contemplation.

There are many books that give help and advice regarding the latter, but the practice of reverse review indicated in the section below ('Preparing for your class', page 21, the 'Rückshau') is a particularly useful part of the toolkit. That itself may be sufficient for some readers, but exercises such as the 'six basics' (sometimes called 'supplementary' exercises) are a great support to good teaching. To take just one of these: a deliberate practice of spending three to five minutes daily maintaining (or trying to maintain) concentration on a single everyday object, following the thoughts that connect logically with that one object, is a huge help to identifying the essentials to present to a class. Just imagine how, after doing this for a week or two with, for example, a pencil as the object, you might well have prepared a entire short lesson about the technology, manufacture and international economics of pencils alongside a moral message. As Einstein put it (and it applies to a pencil as much as to relativity), 'my internal and external life depend so much on the work of others that I must make an extreme effort to give as much as I receive'.

No one unwilling to at least embark on such a course of personal investigation should become a Waldorf class teacher. There are many fine and worthy colleagues who contribute valuably to the life of Waldorf schools, but who stand back from deeper commitment. That is also possible up to the point that the individual assumes direct responsibility for the development of education. Prior to that point, an open-minded, if sometimes grudging, acknowledgement of the logic of Waldorf education is nonetheless indispensable.

In this handbook, I have made sparing but occasional use of some shortcut terms common in Steiner's writing. Words like 'soul and spirit', 'angel' or 'destiny' are no more than tokens of existential encounter. If not identified within your own experience in some way, the accusation that these are quasi-religious symbols becomes an accurate description. On the other hand, say I join my local tennis club and soon after start a campaign to have the nets raised in order to play volleyball instead. My reception is unlikely to be positive. I may complain that the tennis players are set-in-their-ways dogmatists who need to move into the new reforming era of volleyball, but ultimately, I am simply in the wrong place. If Steiner verses, or talk of 'the ego' or 'astral body' are not for you, then joining a Waldorf school becomes the equivalent of ousting the tennis players to promise volleyball.

Every Waldorf teacher has opportunity, through developing personal insight (having started, no doubt, with 'on-sight'), self-training and the 'inner path' of the teacher to be educationally creative. I have indicated a process for curriculum development in the introduction to the fifth English edition of *Rudolf Steiner's Curriculum for Steiner-Waldorf Schools* (the 'Stockmeyer Curriculum')[3] both there and in *The Tasks and Content of the Steiner-Waldorf Curriculum.*[4] In the introduction to the former, these are summarised thus (for a more detailed explanation see the source itself):

* The principle of growth (development and modelling) – relating all learning to the development of the child in order to promote wellbeing and long-term health;
* The principle of life – relating everything the young person learns to life (including to promote feeling for the 'livingness' and life-long learning);
* The principle of empowerment or 'education towards freedom';
* The holistic principle – 'sustainability' including helping to sustain the wonder, joy in learning and curiosity of the child into adulthood;

* The principle of multiple-literacy – a methodology that involves 'economy of teaching', learning through doing and feeling: the integration artistic, experiential and practical learning to sustain intellectual skills;
* The spiritual principle – total respect and care of the unique essence of the growing young person and for the highest possibilities in each of us.

To say that without Rudolf Steiner there would be no Waldorf schools is to state the obvious. Alongside the practical business skills of Emil Molt, Steiner was the inspirer, mentor and sometime critic of the first teachers, who were themselves highly educated and cultured in the science and accomplishments of their time. One hundred years on from that, we are different people with different sensibilities and vulnerabilities. Even the language that we use is more demotic, less formal. The challenge now is to: *Become your OWN Rudolf Steiner!*

That's a collective, not merely a personal, challenge for the Waldorf teacher. It means drinking from the wellsprings of education so that it becomes entirely and authentically our own. We become our own Rudolf Steiner by digesting whatever speaks meaningfully to us from the anthroposophical study of education. In other words, you can explain much of the content of Waldorf education meaningfully to yourself, and live it each in your own distinct and individual way, using the language and culture you have each been given.

The first Waldorf teachers

A little motto

Strength in life, and a sense of humour,
Builds a serious art of education;
A playful learning, constructing what's true,
Is the teacher-learner's firm foundation:
Solid knowledge, though dry to the core
Springs to joyous life through imagination;
Fable and colour in the heart of a learner
Become love through thinking's integration.

We're all learners!

The first teachers were people of their time – and so are we:

Today our teachers cannot know what will be good in the Waldorf School in five years' time, for in those five years they will have learned a great deal and out of that knowledge they have to judge anew what is good and what is not good … Educational matters cannot be thought out intellectually; they can only arise out of teaching experience. And it is this working out of experience that is the concern of the collegiate.[5]

Rudolf Steiner, Arnheim 1924,
Human Values in Education

15

2.

School readiness

In recent years there has been a great deal of work and research into the question of school readiness. While it was once common to think of the question as 'Class One readiness' (and previous editions of this handbook used that term) that title no longer suffices to accurately describe how decisions of this sort need to be made. Class One readiness suggests a single leap from the bed of infancy into the classroom. In fact, the likely impact of decisions made at this transition point work their way out into all levels of schooling including further or higher education.

School readiness involves taking account of many factors including the child's:

* life conditions and background;
* early childhood education;
* family history;
* norms present in law and regulations;
* relevant medical history.

Heeding these factors means we should never treat school readiness simply as a matter of the readiness of the children: the readiness of adults and the school are just as crucial. The key questions are: how can the school meet the needs of the children? And how ready is the teacher?

These questions are an important corrective to any tendency to think of readiness as a simple, linear process: development does not proceed, like travel, along a single-track railway. It is the job of the teacher and the school to adapt to the needs of each child, not to sit passively waiting for the children to be ready by adapting to a notion of what they should be.

Six-year-old blues

Mum sent me to the Steiner
And Kindie's mostly nice,
We play outside all winter
And skid across the ice!

But now I've got a problem:
'I want to go to school!'
All my friends are going
And they say it's really cool.

My teeth are just not wobbling,
I missed the Easter test,
I've even got a special game
To help me with the rest:

I lift my hand,
I tug my arm,
I try to reach my ear;
I think my head is far too big;
I get so very near.

I met the nice class teacher,
She smiled and knew my name,
She even had a chuckle
When I showed her my ear game

I think she really likes me,
She said I was the best,
But she was sad as sad could be
I missed the Easter test!

I lift my hand,
I tug my arm,
I try to reach my ear;
I think my head is far too big:
Now I'll have to wait ONE WHOLE YEAR![6]

There are, nonetheless, useful indicators, that enable the responsible adults to assess how far the development of the individual child has progressed. Decisions such as whether to admit a child into Class One cannot and should not be made simply by using a checklist such as the one that follows. The list is a method that can be used to gather evidence in order to characterise a child more clearly. The process is more a matter of observing and becoming aware. It is *not* a score-card where a certain number of items ticked determine whether the child is offered a place in Class One. All of the points listed here can be observed in the child's normal surroundings, either at home or in Kindergarten. Decisions as to whether a child is ready to leave Kindergarten will have consequences that extend through their schooling and will call on the insights of all of those concerned with the child. These include Kindergarten teacher, the prospective Class One teacher, the College of Teachers, the school doctor and, most importantly, the child's parents. Where there is any doubt, a detailed child study will be necessary, involving considerations other than those listed here. It goes without saying that none of these should be made known to the child (see *Six-year-old blues*, left).

General and non-specific indicators

Date of birth

Research indicates that younger children, referred to as 'summer-born', tend to do less well in all types of formal education than their older cohorts. Some Steiner-Waldorf schools have experimented with creating summer and winter classes, but this is difficult to manage except in larger schools and with double-stream entry. It can be helpful to consider the idea of 'seven Easters', i.e. that the sixth birthday should have been celebrated before Easter. This may be difficult to achieve, but moving the normal point of entry into Class One to May or June has advantages, especially for children who need more time to build social confidence or may be behind others in physical development and other key milestones.

The second dentition

This milestone helps to indicate an aspect of children's physical development. Not only are the second teeth the extrusion of a hard material formed by the individual growth processes of the child, they also gradually change the child's ability to articulate clear consonants such 'd', 't', 'th' and 's'. Ability to form precise sounds is, of course, important for the development of phonological awareness. Remember that the first sign of second dentition is not necessarily the first loose tooth. Before this happens the child usually experiences the eruption of the first adult molars, known as the 'seventh-year molars'. If one or both parents were late in reaching second dentition, less emphasis should be given to this point.

Bodily proportions and characteristics

Differences due to constitutional type should be taken into account. One often has a general impression of the child's appearance and whether bodily proportions are infantile. In general the head/body ratio changes from 1:4 at birth to 1:6 by age six. Loss of baby fat and the 'pot belly' usually occur towards the end of the fifth year. A growth of the legs – the 'first stretching' – generally occurs towards the end of the sixth year.

Gender

Girls' readiness may be apparent sooner than that of boys as they mature earlier. Boys usually grow faster, but develop more slowly. While brain development in girls is quicker than that in boys, whether through genetic or other factors, there may be greater danger of girls 'burning out' academically, leading to an aversion towards school during the teenage years.

Linguistic development in girls tends to start earlier, making academic tasks such as reading and writing more difficult for younger boys. There is a common assumption that boys are more prone to wide variety of learning differences labelled 'dyslexia', but this is not substantiated in recent research where the distinction, although favouring girls by a small margin, was not considered significant. What is important here is to recognise that boys' behaviour tends to draw more attention than that of most girls, and, as a result, boys are more likely to be labelled dyslexic than girls. Not all boys will encounter problems with the usual expectations of a school but, along with girls, a sufficient number means that teachers and schools must plan more radically when shaping activities. Plenty of physical and active time will allow development to take place.

Family

Education is a combined concern of home and schools, and a dialogue between parents and teachers is essential. Families prepare (or fail to prepare their children) for school, and schools need to both support that preparation and be hospitable to what families contribute. Ultimately, growing and learning is a pathway for the unique person the child has the potential to become. The mature individual is thus enabled to form or reform adult relationships in freedom. To achieve this the biological-physical foundation of childhood relationships must transform, and school is one of the mechanisms that society has created to facilitate that process. The partnership between home and school contributes more to readiness for formal learning than is usually recognised, but it must be a partnership in which the role of each contributor is recognised and respected. Ultimately, the school must decide the question of readiness, but decision-making as a command on either side risks leaving the child inwardly split between home and school.

Finally, remember that no item on this checklist should be taken in isolation as the reason for a child starting, or not starting, Class One. The decision should be made 'on balance'.

For further information, Appendix A lists motor proficiency, which will be found useful as background to this, as will detail in Appendix B on 'Warning Signs'.

Checklist: Class One readiness

Physical development

The child would normally show:

* seventh-year molars loose or lost incisor(s);
* can touch top of ear by reaching over top of head with opposite arm, i.e. the changing proportions of head and limbs show lengthening and greater differentiation (remember *Six-year-old blues*, not all children will be able to do this);
* visible waist ('S' curve of the back);
* visible knuckles and kneecaps (instead of dimples);

* arch of foot;
* more defined facial characteristics.

Skills

The child is normally able to:

* throw and catch a large ball;
* hop on either foot;
* jump rhythmically;
* bunny hop (feet together);
* climb, but not necessarily descend, stairs with alternate feet;
* habitually walk swinging the opposite arm to the leading foot, i.e. in cross pattern;
* tie shoes, deal with buttons, zips, etc. (N.B. many of these things will depend upon aspects such as family attitudes and opportunity, etc.);
* look after eating, drinking, washing and toilet needs;
* use fingers dexterously (finger games, use of scissors, finger knot);
* establish laterality (eye and hand are most important; the child may not be conscious of right or left at this stage);
* show a feeling for symmetry as shown in free drawing (not form drawing), e.g., as indicated by the way a face or a house is drawn;
* separate the thumb from the rest of the hand when shaking hands with someone. (It may be noticed in shaking hands with a child that a younger child generally does not separate thumb from fingers but offers the whole hand. School-ready children, provided they know about shaking hands, should offer the hand with the thumb open.)

Social and emotional development

The child will normally:

* join in offered activities;
* share food, toys, their teacher's or parent's attention;
* be willing to take turns;
* help with tasks such as tidying and follow them through;
* not be unduly dependent on a 'comfort' (thumb, blanket, etc.);
* not be regularly an aggressor or victim, accepted by most children in the group (take note of any 'Cinderella' children);
* not be unduly restless or lethargic;
* show indications of reflection, the ability to ponder on an event or impression;
* begin to form friendships based on preference and judgement (not solely on proximity);
* begin to manage feelings and make distinctions in behaviour or speech between different types of people;
* share their dreams with family members or chosen people.

Cognitive development

The child will normally:

* listen to and enjoy stories;
* remember broad outlines of favourite stories;
* talk about recent events coherently, enunciate clearly;
* enjoy songs, rhymes and know some by heart;
* enjoys tricks, schemes and 'cunning plans';
* recognise and name colours;
* be capable of selective attention and concentration on a chosen activity for at least 10–15 minutes;
* be able to run simple errands (remembers and can set a goal);
* have secrets and be able to whisper (distinction between inner and outer);
* use 'linguistic causality' e.g., in sentences starting with 'if' and 'because' (these may be used in word games or imaginative play: 'If we put these logs together they would be higher than the room'). N.B. This is the 'prototype' of the 'causal thinking' that becomes an active much later (age 11–12);
* show in drawing awareness of 'dimensions' in space, blue sky above, green earth below, and placing houses and people near the bottom of the page.

The question of boredom

This is a point that has caused some contention among colleagues. When Kindergarten-age children say they are 'bored' some may assume that this means that children are insufficiently challenged by that environment. In fact 'boredom' frequently indicates something far more significant. Its emergence signifies an inner irritation in a similar way that physical irritation often accompanies bodily development, especially at puberty. Children who never experience boredom because there is always plenty of stimulation are unlikely to take initiative for themselves because the world is too dependable in providing outer distraction. Children who are truly ready for Class One will have gone beyond 'feeling bored' to 'I know a game we can play!' But that is not an easy thing to explain to over-anxious parents.

3.

Preparing for your class

There are as many ways to prepare as there are teachers. Unfortunately there seems to be little guidance for the new teacher and often any sessions dealing with this element during a training course are forgotten by the time the teacher begins to practise. The following is just one possible way to prepare a Morning Lesson, and a similar process can be adopted for other lessons.

The three 'Rs' of preparation:

Readiness ▼ *Review* ▼ *Rehearsal*

Readiness

The motto for the teacher from *Study of Man* is the clue here[7]. We try to create a mood appropriate for a meditative relationship between teacher and class (a relationship of and to spiritual beings).

Work with a verse (the same one for at least half a term or longer) and a further five or ten minutes of meditative study (a lecture from *Study of Man* or material in *Towards a Deepening...* might be appropriate). I would suggest reading no more than one or two paragraphs to focus clearly on

a main thought that can be held in mind for a moment or two before turning to the following stages. You will find that the activity works on, and has consequences for, one's teaching far beyond the time spent on it.

Review

Before looking ahead, it is essential to look back on the previous lesson. Try to follow the sequence of events precisely and in order (or in *Rückshau*) but without judgement. Then consider the following (thanks to Els Göttens and Rosemary Gebert, from whose work this list is adapted):

1. Did I bring real and appropriate images to the class to convey what I wanted to teach? (N.B. an image is not a judgement or concept). What images can I prepare for tomorrow?

2. Did I bring something new – a skill or some knowledge – or some variation on an existing theme? Did I use an image to give this to the children? What shall I bring anew tomorrow?

3. Did I ensure the children had an opportunity to revivify the content of the previous day's

lesson? Did I use the night? How shall I ensure that today's lesson is properly recalled? What will be carried over to a third day? (See two-day, three-day rhythm on page 78.)

4. Has *every* child made at least some effort and did they have time to apply that effort? If not, why not? How shall I stimulate that child tomorrow?

5. Did I make use of the language of temperaments today so that each child felt addressed? How shall I do so tomorrow?

6. Have I used every opportunity to get the children to move (i.e. do first, understand later)? How shall I translate what I wish to teach into movement tomorrow?

7. Was there an ebb and flow, a real breathing, in the lesson: listening/doing; seriousness/gaiety; movement/stillness; sadness/laughter? (N.B. a lesson without laughter is a lost lesson – but so is one where there is *only* laughter.) How shall I plan tomorrow's lesson so that it and the class can breathe?

It does not take long to carry through a review of this sort and it provides plenty of potential material for the next day.

N.B. The question is not simply 'what must I, as teacher, do tomorrow?', but, 'how will my doing encourage the class to become active in their learning so that they increasingly learn for themselves and for one another?'.

Rehearse

New poems, songs and exercises will need to be practised as they will be done in the class. Variations also need to be practised and explored (it is in the doing that possible variations emerge).

The aim should be to be confident in placing these before the class and assured enough to be able to adapt or explore a new aspect that presents itself. Some teachers also write and illustrate their own Morning Lesson book. This can be valuable, especially with a new class. It is time-consuming but the effort can be worth it for the confidence that it engenders. However, it is advisable not to make a habit of putting this in front of the class while they work as this invites over-dependence and could be discouraging for some children. But it could be an occasional reference for the class to come and inspect when they have finished their work, or to get ideas when 'stuck'. Blackboard demonstration, allowing the class to see a picture or example built up before their eyes, is probably the most effective teaching aid. With a particularly careless or undisciplined class, the teacher's activity in this aspect can make a considerable difference.

A story will probably need additional practice (summarise, read before sleep and recap the following morning). It is best to do all possible background reading for the coming year during the summer break, so that the images and their deeper meaning can mature in the mind before they are needed.

For any Morning Lesson, all three stages need take no more than an hour; it is possible to complete this in 45 minutes. It is my belief that without these three elements being present in some form during the preparation, the process will be inadequate.

And the fourth 'R'!

The *Rückshau*, 'reverse review', or the 'daily rewind', was referred to above and some readers of the earlier edition have asked for further information to be included here. Unfortunately there seems to be no elegant alternative in English to the German word, so we will continue to use the latter as a technical term. There are many reference sources for the *Rückshau* in Steiner's work and elsewhere (e.g. *Occult Science*, pp 251-252, 1979 edition, Rudolf Steiner Press). As with so many other exercises of this sort, it is fairly easy to describe, but difficult to do. Especially at the end of a tiring day, the danger is that sleep sucks one in, so it may be best not to leave it until too late.

Previously, I suggested making a *Rückshau* of Morning Lesson as an introduction to the 'review' part of the above preparation process and to take a small section of the day, even one activity, and to try to picture the whole procedure in reverse; doing this can prove to be both strengthening and entertaining.

Imagine watching yourself brushing your teeth up to the moment the small snake of toothpaste withdraws itself back into the tube. It can help to have a picture of what you are imagining. For some, the idea of rewinding a video tape might help, others approach it by imagining looking back from the top of a hill with the events of the day laid out in order below, or some visualise themselves physically moving through time from the evening to the start of the day. Whichever approach works best is the one for you.

What cannot be emphasised enough is that one has to be careful not to fall into the understandable temptation, either in imagining how you *would* have liked a particular encounter to have unfolded, or to begin giving yourself moral ticks and crosses. Starting with what appear to be neutral events can help to establish a good habit for the exercise, but I have found when my attention slips and I find myself 'thinking about' rather than 'picturing', it can be helpful to deliberately hold the last image in mind for a moment as a freeze-frame and try to recreate all the incidental details. This can be supported in the way that one pictures events, especially when with others, as though from the outside (imagine yourself as the objective narrator of classic novel). Painful events, or ones that arouse strong emotion in other ways, once they have been freeze-framed, can then also be placed into the lap of sleep, with a prayer towards the wisdom (and possibly repentance) of the following morning. Call it what you will – the work of your angel, the wisdom of the night or even 'cognitive digestion' if you prefer.

The plan: having and holding an intention

To educate without intention is to educate without purpose, but, as Wiseacres[8] warns, 'The road to perdition is paved with good intentions' have to remember that intention needs to be more than a brilliant idea.

In order to work on a practical level, intentions call for a plan of action. This is what the planning forms in this handbook are intended to help with. But plans can be explicit or implicit, and the implicit plan of an experienced teacher, based on thousands of previous lessons, must not be allowed to distract us from the necessity of planning as such. In fact, good explicit planning can enhance learning through trial and error.

An explicit plan aids you, but it can also help your colleagues, especially if for some reason you are unable to teach the lesson you have planned. It is also a vital ingredient for effective mentoring, as 'dry-mentoring', working with a lesson that is still only in plan, can be as useful as lesson observation. Without a written plan there is a danger that the best teaching ideas simply evaporate. A well-constructed plan enables deeper consideration and focuses action, principally by setting out learning objectives and means to achieve them. Good planning also eases the way for learning itself and for evaluation. Planned learning outcomes can be readily entered into a record of individual pupil progress and the plan will always allow the creative teacher to find a more powerful alternative to achieving memorable learning in the moment.

The plans below are examples of the craft, and graft, that the art of education needs. These examples are not intended to be exemplary, or to be used for teaching. They are included here purely for illustrative purposes.

An annual plan

You will need to set out how you intend to distribute lessons and lesson themes throughout the year. The planner in this handbook provides for a general overview, the merest sketch of topics alongside things you may have to take into account, for example, school festivals (see sample opposite).

SAMPLE: *Class 4 Annual Plan*

Date (autumn)	4 weeks	4 weeks	4 weeks[9]	4 weeks
Theme	**Our town**	**Number work**	**Norse sagas – literacy**	**Term review**
Summary	Local history. Geography. Introduction to mapping.	First step to fractions. Times table patterns revised. Form drawing. Active introduction to concept leading to X fractions. Concept of 'half of'. Link to concepts of measurement.	Ginnungagap to the nine worlds. Vanir to Æsir to Norns. The birth of language. Metaphor and simile. Riddles. Use of basic tenses. Direct and reported speech. Simple descriptive grammar. 'Knot-work' patterns.	Practice and recap. Check. Embed all skills.
Comments	Autumn. Harvest festivals.	Assembly.	Winter. Midwinter festivals. Introduce Class play.	End of term assembly.

Date (winter–spring)	Spring term – 3 weeks	4 weeks	3 weeks	1 week
Theme	**Fractions**	**Zoology (human and animal)**	**Mind your language**	**Revise and evaluate**
Summary	Building on introductory work. Use of LCM. Factor analysis. Proper and improper fractions. Mixed numbers. Simplifying and expanding. Version of Eratosthenes' sieve. Calculating + (plus) and – (minus) as well as x (multiply) and ÷ (divide), for example 'How many halves in 13 ÷ 4?'	Overview picture of human systems such as nerve-sense, cardio-respiratory, muscle-metabolic. Fundamental gestures of animal forms. Correspondence between form and environment/condition. Modelling, painting and illustration.	Types of writing. 'Expressive pictures' as found in Old English and Norse. For example 'the swan's riding' = the sea. Clear directions and instructions. Alliteration. Use of a dictionary and thesaurus. Simple and elaborate sentences. Parts of speech. Letter forms. Development of language and script, such as Ogham letters, runes, modern script, Norse-style script. Book of spelling rules.	Check progress (are all books completed?) and reinforce key objectives.
Comments	New Year.	Mid-term. To include a simple 'project' such as a study of pet or animal in the immediate environment. Short presentations to class.	Spring festival. Play rehearsals.	End of Term festival. Perform Class Play.

Date (spring–summer)	3 weeks	4 weeks	4 weeks	2 weeks
Theme	**Arithmetic**	**Celts, Saxons and Norsemen**	**Work in our region**	**Revise and evaluate**
Summary	Revise and extend all fractions: include tenths and hundredths. Metric system (prep. for decimals). Time. Measurement (such as MPH) of the rate of increase and decrease. Ratio.	Tales of the Western Isles. Britain and Ireland. People and folk history. Norse 'end of time'. Norna-Gest saga.	Link to local geography and history, for example, services and businesses important in the town and region. Crafts and skills. 'People who help us' (emergency services). Transport. Communications.	Preparing books to be taken home. A full evaluation of the year's work. A 'taster' of Class Five.
Comments	Early summer.		Mid-summer festival. Field trips. Journal writing. Illustrating.	End of term.

An overview plan for Morning Lesson

You will need an overview plan for the morning lesson and for other lessons taught in a block, which might include lessons such as handwork, crafts or gardening. You can set out how the various topics, skill building and practice will be distributed across the block with some detail of activities and approach.

SAMPLE: *'Our Town' (first week only – make a similar plan for weeks 2, 3 and 4, if available)*

Monday	Tuesday	Wednesday	Thursday	Friday
Brief intro	Brief intro	Quality work for speech. Poem. Practice key sounds and add to instrumental work. Explore 'sounds of our town'.	Continue from previous. Extend and improve.	Sum up from week. What still needs practice?
Rhythmic	Work on 'Our Town' and compass game		**Recall:** Cornmarket Lane. Any others?	Perform.
'Here are we'. Folk songs from area. Compass points exercise. Instrumental work. 'Our Town' poem.	**Recall story:**	**Recall yesterday:** What's interesting about our town? Why is it here?	Group work to recall 10 things about our town and using scale.	**Week's recall:**
Birthday verses.	Yesterday's maps: What's missing? Could someone who didn't know the journey follow it? What does it show of the town?	Create a written description to go with 'map'. Check and write.	**Activity:** Precise plan of classroom to simple scale (group work).	**Completing work from week**
About our town: Discussion about features of the town, where class members live and their journey to class.	Improved versions of sketch maps for books showing more information. Naming areas of the town.	**Mapping activity:**	Writing clear directions from your house to school (for books).	Get books up-to-date.
Sketch a map from your house to school, showing landmarks.	**Spelling** patterns based on these. Describe journey in words. Prep for unusual or distinctive road names.	Map the classroom and the building. Using plan-view. Using scale, explore what it is, when is it used and why?	Spelling list using place and road names.	**Spelling quiz**
Share and discuss		Other places you know with similar names or elements (quick **spelling** aspect)	Other places you know with similar names or elements (quick **spelling** aspect).	**Celebrate work accomplished**
Spelling exercise with name of town		**Story**: 'Cornmarket Lane'	**Rivers, hills and who lived here before us?** Investigation for tomorrow.	**A local legend**
Create title page: for Morning Lesson books. Share these.				Preparation for geographical history next week.
Story: A legend from the town.				
Check journey for tomorrow				

A daily lesson plan

A daily lesson plan sets out the 'management' of the lesson, teaching and learning.

We have included two types of format for this: first, a 'standard version'; second, a 'mind map' version:

Teachers may have their own methods of recording their preparation. Sometimes these consist of a detailed list of items for the Morning Lesson, but sometimes there is little else. The forms that follow are not intended to replace personal notes. Instead they provide an overview of the lesson and day ahead with points for reminders in an accessible form: these are to be used as a lesson management tool. Plans of this sort can be modified as needed and provide a valuable daily record of the main activities of each day in a form that takes very little time to maintain.

The key is, the more immediate plan to lesson, the greater the detail. However, to borrow a cliché from Ofsted pronouncements (sometimes hard to avoid) what is needed is a 'well planned lesson'. A well-written lesson plan is no substitute for that, and is at best an abstract curiosity unless it assists effective teaching and learning in the classroom.

SAMPLE: Morning Lesson plan – standard version

Date:	Class:	Subject:	Teacher:
Rhythmic work	**Outcomes/criteria**	**Skills**	**Observations**
Practice			
Work arising			
Narrative			
Differentiation			
Materials			
Evaluation			

Quick lesson planner

Class: Teacher: Date:

The BIG picture?

Your Major aim!

'To unite the bodily physical & soul-spiritual'!

Objectives

What do you hope to achieve this lesson?

Engagement?

Points of departure to interest and involve

Stickers!

Aids to remember key points

Formative assessments

What I'm looking for: how will you know you (student) have succeeded?

Celebrate/review next lesson

Exercises leading to: Process, rhythm, recall...

Written work

2: academic

Differentiation

Extras: children to support or will need more challenge

Practice pieces: Mental arithmetic, spelling exercise, etc.

Illustration/map or...

Learning episodes 1: practical/artistic

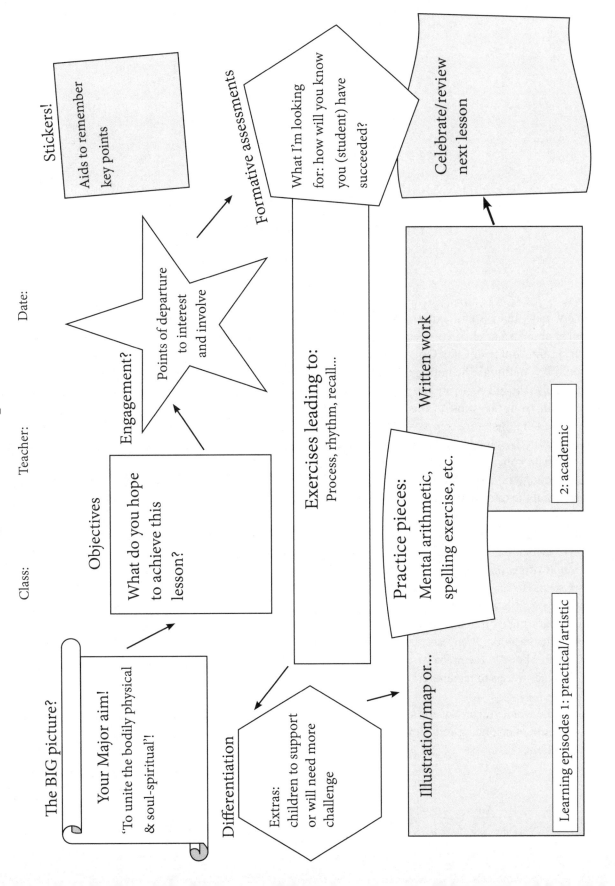

4.

Setting aims and objectives for Class One

Many new (and some experienced) colleagues worry about what children need to have grasped during the course of Class One. A simple answer would be, 'nothing'. The nothing, however, in this case is also the full circle, an 'eternity within a span'. After all, 'from the whole to the parts' means that in Class One the entire compass of the successive curriculum is contained, fortunately, in picture rather than concept, and in feeling and will rather than through intellect. But the foundations for the habits and the tone of the class in subsequent years will be set in the first ones, even though the children initially appear impervious. Many an experienced class teacher has said goodbye to Class One in a mood of pessimism, only to greet a Class Two that seems to have been temporarily transformed into angels. It is a fact worth remembering during those dark nights that threaten to obliterate many a summer vacation. Even lesser transformations do not come about by themselves.

Two key things to remember:

* **Smile** when you meet a child's gaze. It creates a sense of belonging and shows you like being with the class.

* **Know their names** – for a new class, obtain photographs and learn names before they start with you. If necessary, print the photographs small size with names attached and use as a crib.

The following is a list of questions and hints that may help you at the start of your voyage of discovery.

On the first day

Is the classroom ready for the class? Is it clean, tidy, decorated, polished and with some seasonal plants and fruits?

* Do all the children in the class know where the toilets are? (An opportunity to remind about washing hands – especially as this will no doubt feature in the first lesson.)
* There will probably be an assembly (perhaps one of the older classes will make a presentation to Class One – is this prepared?), parents will probably want to stay around longer than usual and tell you all sorts of last-minute, important information. Have some small, easily arranged activity prepared that the children can do after you have greeted

them. (Drawing works well. You might keep the drawings as part of your file as interesting pointers for the future.)

* Young children like to know where they are in the world. It will assist the children's sense of security if they know you have thought about where they will hang their coats and where they will sit.

* Without overburdening the children with a list of explicit rules, the class should feel themselves to be in a disciplined environment. In passing, the teacher can indicate such things as, 'in Class One we do not run along the corridor', 'you may write on my blackboard, when I say you can', or 'to make sure I can hear every one of you when you have something you want to say in class, you can put up your hand first', etc.

* Speak about the morning verse, but introduce it on the second day (perhaps it will have been spoken during the opening assembly).

* Have you prepared a few activities you can use 'just in case'? (Things will never work out quite as you expect.)

* Have you read Chapter 4 of *Practical Advice…*? (Too late to do so now if you haven't!) Have you thought about how much you can realistically do on the first day? (It may be far less than you expect.)

* Think about the balance between speaking to the class and what they will be doing. Don't keep them sitting and listening for too long. An outdoor activity, such as bulb planting, provides opportunity to ensure coats and changes of shoes are understood. (Are there tools available? Do you know where to plant and how much space will be needed?)

* A 'short day' for Class One's start is generally advisable.

* Parents will certainly want to talk to you at the end of the first day (not for the last time, one hopes) and some children may need to wait longer, so again, end-of-school activities (cleaning, putting-away, etc) may be useful.

* In general prepare more than you need, but expect not to use most of it.

* Enjoy the day.

By the end of the first year

* The children should feel safe and secure in the classroom and in school (see above).

* The teacher should not do for the class anything the children should be able to do for themselves (e.g., setting up for painting, cleaning the classroom, giving out books). The children should feel that they are self-reliant, though the teacher's presence will usually still be needed to sustain this.

* Circle time should be purposeful with a range of balanced and progressive activities.

* All children should be taking part in all the activities of the class – exceptions should be rare.

* Members of the class should be able to (usually) sit together in most combinations of position in the class without disruption

* The children should willingly offer to shake hands in the morning.

* Outdoor routines for walks, etc., 'stopping places', safety for road crossing, etc., 'country code', 'return to teacher signal' should be all well established and observed.

* The class members should take pride in their own work and the children freely express appreciation of the work of others.

* Put-downs between children should be rare or non-existent.
* The rhythm of Morning Lesson and other lessons should be well-established – the children will know what to expect and help to maintain this.
* Good classroom habits should be now be done without prompting: e.g. hanging up coats, changing shoes, looking after crayons, books and other classroom materials, changing into painting smocks, safety routines for walks, saying of grace before meals, staying at places during meal breaks until the class or individuals are dismissed, choral speaking of verses, use of waste paper/compost bins, visits to the bathroom during lessons are not frequent and non-disruptive, notes to and from home are delivered.
* Beginnings and ends of lessons are observed (e.g., class stands when new teacher enters the room).
* Class One items from the other checklists.

The above list is intended only as an indication. Each teacher and every school may have slightly different requirements. But it is important to know what yours are. And, for a new teacher, it is important that a mentor or companion makes sure the new colleague knows what the norms are in that particular school. Clear policies are essential.

Things to consider when setting specific learning outcomes (LOUTS):

* So far as possible, write them in a form and words that, when spoken, the children will understand.
* 'We will learn...' rather than, 'we will be writing/making/drawing...'
* How will you – and they – know they have achieved what is intended?
* Are learning intentions manageable, accessible and visible?
* How can you involve the pupils? Why should they feel that these outcomes are worth the effort?
* Have you a clear sense for the process you will be involving the class in?

5.

Recording
and self-evaluation

The checklists included in this book give an indication of what we might expect children to feel secure with in each class stage. The teacher will need to keep a record of what children can do, but where a whole class is falling a long way behind in a number of areas, he or she should use the information to ask whether their lack of ability is a reflection of the teaching. (Can one say the children have been *taught* if they have not learned?)

It is advisable for a number of colleagues to work together to support one another in this process, sharing aims and problems as they arise. Any targets for attainment will vary to some extent according to the children concerned. The teachers' group would do well to spend time over what would be the 'normal' expectation in their school. ('Normal' is used here, as before, to indicate a general level of expectation, which, though it will certainly vary in reality, should be as high as possible.)

Record keeping can easily be a hit-or-miss affair, with school policies sometimes overly dependent on the discretion, and experience, of individual teachers. A Waldorf teacher will work hard to maintain a vivid developmental picture of each child: how much have they grown

during the year; have there been changes in their physiognomy, complexion and voice, are they getting fat or thin? But in order to remember which multiplication tables the children really know (or to be sure of this in the first place), and whether a particular child makes certain characteristic mistakes in spelling, these things require some record keeping. This should not, however, lead to a time-consuming, intrusive activity. It will be found helpful to have a folder of representative work (including some first drafts with spelling and grammatical errors clearly marked). This need contain no more than two or three pieces of work per term. In addition, there is a need to record what basic skills and knowledge the children have attained.

The key to this is simplicity: there should be no unnecessary information. The material will be mainly for your benefit, but should be recorded efficiently to ensure that it can be clearly understood by another adult without the need for extensive explanation. This makes things much easier if, for some reason, another teacher has to take over the class (see Appendices C to F) and makes writing reports much less of a chore. It goes without saying that a short account of the Morning Lessons covered and their content should also be kept (see Section Two, Chapter 8: Curriculum and basic skills). Class teachers might do well to ask of themselves: 'What information would I need, and what would be available, if I were a teacher taking over the class at short notice'. Waldorf teachers do well to remember that we are all mortal, and life situations sometimes change unexpectedly and at short notice.

N.B. A hat-tip with thanks to colleagues at Wynstones Steiner School, who did as I had intended and reworked my original checklists. Here I borrow back and rework what they did.

6.

Checklists for
Classes One to Three

The following checklists are for skills we might expect children to develop during Classes One, Two and Three. Records for the classes have been assumed. By Class Three (I would recommend by spring term) the teacher should be in a position to carry out a detailed assessment of the progress of the class and, through this, a realistic self-assessment of the teaching itself (preferably in association with colleagues).

Skills checklist

Child:		Class:		Teacher:	
Class	**Checklist item**	**Achieved**	**Comments – exceeded or not acheived (how?)**	**Proposed action**
E.g. 1	Demonstrate appreciation of number qualities	See note[10]		
and	Count accurately to 100	Date each		
and	Demonstrate accurate one-to-one correspondence			
and	Recognise the whole and different parts (e.g 10 = 5+5; and also 3+7)			

Numeracy

One: Demonstrate an appreciation of number qualities, 1–10 or 1–12.

One: Count accurately to 100 (and more) and count from 100–0 (reverse sequence) with confidence.

One: Be able to associate number with relevant quantity.

One: Demonstrate whole number (e.g. 10) in various arrangements of parts (9+1, 2+8).

One: Identify quantity through direct recognition and pattern (e.g. patterns used on a die or for playing cards) especially…

One: …Recognising numbers shown by hand (including variations, e.g. 7 with 5 on the left hand and 2 on the right, then 4 on left and 3 on the right, etc.Show a working knowledge of +, –, × and ÷ as process and as symbol in verbal and written form.

One: Confidently count in twos, threes, fives and tens(this is not to be confused with knowledge of times tables).

Two: Recite (by heart) addition and subtraction facts in the region of 20 (number bonds).

Two/Three: Read correctly and be able to 'analyse' numbers up to at least thousands (e.g., 243 as 'two hundred and forty-three' or 'two hundred, four tens and three units').

One–Three: Know what follows 99, 999, 9999, etc. (In Class One, check none of the children are counting, e.g., 'thirty-nine, fourteen… forty-nine, fifteen', etc.

One: Addition and subtraction 'facts' by heart in the region of twenty (number bonds).

Two: Can demonstrate the difference between odd and even numbers

Two: Know multiplication tables 1 to 10 at least (both in order and out of sequence).

Two/Three: Know these as division (not only that 6 × 4 is 24 and 24 is 4 × 6, but also that 24 ÷ 6 = 4, etc.)

Three: Appreciate tricks (patterns) of 10× table; 9, 5, 11, etc.)

Two: Understand differences between odd and even numbers.

Two/Three: Use place value in the range of 4 places correctly, i.e. show practical understanding that the 1 in 1, 12 and 138, etc. has different values.

Two/Three: Be able to 'carry numbers' (i.e. proper use of place value) for + (e.g., 19 + 2) and × (e.g., 74 × 2).

Two/Three: Tell time, at least hours, half-past, and quarter-past (N.B. The analogue clock should be learned first).

Two/Three: Subtract from 'smaller units' (e.g., 12 – 9); at this stage this is best done by decomposition – (from whole to part).

One–Three: Do simple mental arithmetic in narrative form relating to above skills.

Three: Count to 1,000 – also in reverse!

Two/Three: Be able to use money correctly for simple bills and calculating change, etc.

Three: Be able to calculate simple 'pre-area' sums such as how many milk bottles will be in a crate of bottles holding six by six using simple calculations, or size of wall or floor on basis of number of bricks or tiles.

N.B. All the above are needed before fractions can be efficiently tackled.

Form drawing

One–Three: Do freehand drawings of common geometric forms (as a dynamic drawing rather than precise forms).

One/Two: Have a sense for symmetrical completion of forms on upright axis (early in Class One) and as horizontal reflections.

Three: Be able to complete 'complex' symmetries including left/right, above/below with crossing at mid-point – a certain maturity is needed for this. (Assuming the children have crossed the nine-year Rubicon).

Literacy

One: Prepare for writing: look, listen, wake up hands, sit ready. Use correct tripod grip for writing. Copy sentences accurately.

One: Read and understand what the class has written in the classroom.

One: Read own written work confidently.

One/Two: Spell own name and address.

One/Two: Read a number of poems or songs known to the class.

One: Recognise sounds of all vowels and consonants and sound them appropriately…

One/Two: …for both capital and lower case letters.

Two: Know names of letters.

Two/Three: Know alphabetical order of letters.

Two/Three: Recognise cursive and printed form of letters.

Two/Three: Know the sounds of:
* consonant blends * (st, sp, tr, etc.);
* vowel digraphs * (ee, oo, ai, etc.) (*see Appendix B for these);
* vowel/consonant digraphs (ow, ew, aw);
* vowels + r (as in: er, ar, or), diphthongs (oy, oi);
* consonant digraphs (sh, th, ch, wh, ng);

One/Two: Make a good attempt to sound out unknown words showing knowledge of phonics.

One/Two: Know, and can write, days of the week, months, numbers.

One–Three: Write simple accounts of a recent event (e.g., diary), or a well-known story with commonly used words spelled correctly and make sensible attempts at more complicated words.

One/Two: Know commonly used irregular words, e.g., 'was', 'are', 'said', 'have'.

One/Two: Read random lines of text and in reverse order.

Two/Three: Read unknown text equal in difficulty to 'Hay for my Ox' with reasonable confidence.

Two/Three: Use full stops and capital letters.
Three: Write 'thank you' letters.
Three: Cursive handwriting should be well formed by this time, with a good balance of the three zones and no 'short-cut' formations such as:

Other skills

Class

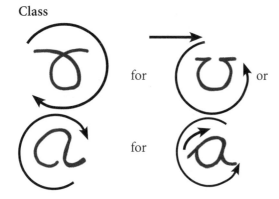

for ... or

for

One: Recite in chorus and speak short verses alone.
One–Three: Accompany poem with fluent and appropriate gestures.
One/Two: Imitate simple pentatonic melody.
Three: Sing in tune and with correct rhythm; have a repertoire of known songs and play them on a flute/recorder.
Three: Follow unknown melody indicating rise and fall with hand/arm movements.
Three: Identify well-known tunes from rhythm alone.
Two: Prepare for painting without assistance. Grade colours by adjusting dilution. Paint cleanly.

Two–Three: Know combination of primary colours to produce secondary.
One–Three: Recognise and name common trees and plants (especially those in locality).
One–Three: Know which local plants are hazardous (N.B. Through nature stories, games, etc., and not the 'Observer's Book' approach).
Three: Speak clearly individually in recitation (N.B. all children of this age should be able to roll the 'r').
Three: Recognise the major food crops.
Two–Three: Use scissors accurately.
One–Three: Be able to plan and prepare, e.g., a simple moving picture.
Two–Three: Be able to finger-knit, knit with needles, crochet, reasonable facility in sewing.
Two: Be able to model a variety of forms in free work using plasticine or wax from whole ball to resemblance of required figure.

N.B. the objectives for mathematics differ from those to be found in Ron Jarman's *Teaching Mathematics*. The two lists are complementary. The latter is appropriate as a guide to teaching content and aspiration; the checklists are intended as minimum attainments for most children of normal ability in the class concerned.

N.B. Ideally, by the end of Class Three children should have begun to learn another appropriate musical instrument.

7.

Imitation

The first three classes are, from one point of view, the most important as far as the class teacher is concerned. It is during this time that the habits of the class, which have their basis in the ether body, are laid down. It is helpful for the teacher to have thought out what the essentials are, the foundations for good working habits that children will need all their school years. Better to have these already in mind than to find yourself reacting to undesirable or disruptive behaviour and trying to control it once already established.

That is where the residue of imitation, which the children bring with them from Kindergarten, provides the first support for the teacher. Remember how much time and effort goes into creating the right environment in pre-school work. It is as well not to cast Kindergarten child-of-habit out with the Class One wash water. Unless the class teacher observes a certain orderliness and beauty in the arrangement of the classroom, the children are unlikely to recreate it themselves in their own work and learning. While some of the forms and customs of Kindergarten will need to change, the habit of hanging up coats and changing shoes will still be needed in Classes Six, Seven and Eight. If the soul yearns for the beautiful, the reluctant body may be moved to create it.

Imitation, however, is not the most important tool for the class teacher and we know that today fewer children retain a natural imitative faculty until the ninth or tenth year. What must replace this during the school years is the discipline of being at school (discipline – discipleship). The teacher creates a social environment in which certain forms of behaviour are expected. One soon finds the children themselves can become the most effective conservers of the norms of the class, provided they feel they have a real stake in maintaining those norms. A feeling that the class is learning and growing together, that each one has invested something of themselves in creating the mood and physical appearance of the class, is the essence of this. It amounts to transforming the outer imitative faculty into a sort of soul imitation, a feeling motivation. In Kindergarten the world is adapted to the child, but in the Upper School the students begin to adapt themselves to the world. During the class–teacher period these two are in a dynamic tension; the world is experienced through the adult so that children begin to model themselves according to what is living in the teacher.

Circle time

I suspect there are few class teachers who have not at some time found themselves working hard to do an exercise with the class only to notice that a number of the children are either moving in a vague imitation of what was intended or are more involved in trying to pester the child in front. This, (and it becomes worse the more energetically the teacher tries to continue), is a common scene during 'circle time' and can lead to movement becoming no more than a moment or two of self-conscious physical jerks before a largely desk-bound lesson.

If we consider more seriously the transition from imitation to discipline, we might see that it is more effective for a teacher to show an exercise for the class to absorb inwardly alongside some images. These figures can help the children comprehend the essential elements of the task. When the class or small group then do what they have seen, the teacher is more able to guide and direct the activity.

8.

Observation

'Observe the children' ought to be the motto inscribed on every teacher's desk. Not having time to do this may be the symptom of a nervous teacher (and subsequently a nervous class).

Ultimately the aim is that the children take on the activity, developing variations of their own and providing the teacher with new insights into what they need. The process of teaching is one in which the teacher is endlessly seeking to become redundant.

Whose classroom is it?

A naïve observer in the classroom might ask the question: 'Why does the teacher spend the lesson prowling up and down in front of the class when not sitting at the teacher's desk?' (some teachers rarely sit down at all).

For teachers who are on their feet the whole lesson, the question to ask is: 'When do you give yourself opportunity to observe what is happening?

If you are busy throughout the lesson, when will you see how your students are engaging with their tasks?'

For 'prowlers' at the front: 'Do you think you are marking territory? Surely the whole classroom space is there for your teaching, so why not use it?'

When you move around the classroom while giving instructions, or speaking to the class you get different 'looks' at what is going on, the children feel your presence and you are making it clear that you are not held captive in a non-existent spotlight. This applies while telling stories (especially after Class One) and describing the Battle of Nasby as much as it does while the class work on their books. More to the point, you are making sure that when you do have to step into the class it is not a novelty, implying that you have been forced to leave the teacher's spot to enter the student-occupied sector!

The following sections have arisen from a number of questions posed to the Advisory Circle. Take from them whatever may be helpful.

9.

Movement skills for
Classes One to Four

The modern world encourages passivity. As a result the body becomes too heavy for the soul to carry, so when puberty comes the body is experienced increasingly as a clumsy obstacle. The teaching of good movement skills provides a basis (in children's habits – which have been inscribed into the ether body) for an active engagement with the world. By consciously cultivating movement skills throughout the eight classes the class teacher can do much to remedy adolescent lethargy, a state that readily leads to its opposite of violent, meaningless movement.

Lists of standard skills for Class One through to Class Four can be found below. The class teacher needs to find imaginative means to develop these skills. However, teachers should be firm in holding their expectations and in recording the children's achievements. They provide as much a basic vocabulary for bodily development as literacy and numeracy do for intellectual progress.

The following lists introduce a series of externalised balance and sensory integration skills (for more details refer to Appendix A on page 93).

Class One movement skills checklist

The aim should be that all children join in movement exercises.

* Good body geography ('Head shoulders knees and toes', 'Simon says').
* Throwing to oneself – bean bags, balls.
* Throwing and catching to each other (age seven onwards).
* Clapping above and below legs (sitting, standing and walking).
* Singing and action games, circle games
* Skipping, both as basic 'dance steps' and rope skipping.
* Writing with the foot (should be legible by Class Two).
* Jumping over obstacles (a rope at increasing heights).
* String games, particularly where one hand has string and the other is active in manipulating the string.

Class Two movement skills checklist

The aim is that all children do the exercises well, in both small groups and as a class.

* Clap in front of and behind body.
* Catch beanbag with different parts of the body (under chin, below other arm, between the legs, etc.)
* Walk over a balance beam or stepping stones (can be combined with a verse or rhyme).
* Follow a line on the floor while balancing a bean bag on head.
* Do exact rhythmic clapping.
* Write with foot, which should be legible (also picking up acorns with toes and placing in a bucket – this could be done as a race).
* Walk on toes and heels to develop a sense for placing of the foot.
* Play aiming games (through legs and passing over heads when children in a row, balls or bean bags into a container, rings onto sticks, etc.)
* See-saw together (a frightened child can be placed in the middle).
* Play hopscotch, bowling hoops, tops, etc.
* Do more complex string games ('cat's cradle').

Classes Three and Four movement skills checklist

The aim should be that every child can do exercises properly, both independently and in groups.

* Walk on a balance beam, with a bean bag or rod on head (with the beam at chair or desk level).
* Pass one another on a beam or tree trunk (without pushing one another off).
* Skip in sequence (skip, hop, twirl, etc.)
* Take part in team games involving co-operation.
* Clap complicated patterns (cross-clapping in pairs).
* Walk on stilts.
* March in patterns (four steps forward, turn to right, one step, turn left…)
* Do the crab walk (ask child to squat down, reach backwards and put both hands on the floor behind without sitting down. Keep head, neck and body in a straight line).

10.

Classes Four and Five checklists

Class Five is a busy year, but a good point at which to take stock. (The checklist for this class of course includes many items covered during Class Four.) In new or smaller schools, Class Five may also be the best point for class to end. Without a real wave to crest full classes below, it is better to aim to prepare the children to join secondary education at this stage, rather than for the class to experience the 'lame duck' syndrome, where children leave gradually and the uncertainty undermines the lower classes.

Realistic decisions need to be made at this point. Children between 9 and 11 like to acquire facts, and this is often the age of collections. The following checklist also includes a number of indications regarding content, facts and figures, that they will continue to cultivate during the following school years and that provide much of the general knowledge that a firm relationship with the surrounding world requires.

Towards the end of Class Five the class will normally be able to do the following.

Numeracy

Four/Five:	Carry out all four processes of number confidently and in other number bases, e.g., yards, feet and inches, etc. (N.B. It is not necessary to teach the binary system abstractly, but rather to use concrete examples such as imperial measures or the Inuit counting system using base 5).
Four:	Read and analyse numbers up to and beyond six figures.
Five:	Apply similar principles to decimal fractions, i.e. 0.1, 0.01, 0.001, etc.
Four/Five:	Answer more complex mental arithmetic questions involving a mix of processes, both in 'narrative' form and as 'number gym' (e.g. A train from Stourbridge Junction to New Street is due to leave at 15.09 and arrive at 15.30; it actually arrives at 15.59, by how much was it delayed? Or: I doubled a number and added 8 and got 32, what was the number?).
Four:	Find factors of a given number.
Four:	Identify prime numbers less than 100
Four:	Find lowest common denominator of highest common factor of group of numbers or more.

Four: Record information such as heights, weights, etc., in a class (using bar charts, for example).

Four: Calculate long multiplication and division sums with numbers up to 100 as multiple or divisor, check by reverse process.

Five: Use the 'rule of three' (£2.50 to buy 10 pencils, how much for 8?)

Five: Carry out four processes with decimals (addition and subtraction observing decimal point, and multiplication and division where multiplier and divisor is a whole number).

Four/Five: Estimate approximate answers (as needed for long division especially).

Four/Five: Apply four processes with fractions, including mixed numbers.

Four: Estimate measurement.

Five: Calculate area of squares, rectangles, triangles and irregular forms by resolving them into simpler shapes.

Five: Know time, including 24-hour clock and processes in time, e.g., miles per hour; e.g. driving at 70 mph on a motorway (N.B. speed limits) how many miles will I travel in two hours and twelve minutes?

Four/Five: Draw more complicated 'Celtic' and similar types of 'knotwork' in form drawing and reproduce forms from ancient civilisations.

Five: Create own version based on the originals.

Four: Produce freehand geometry with reasonable accuracy.

Five: Use ruler and compass accurately, 'Greek' geometry (but only after plenty of freehand work.)

Five: Draw, recognise and name different common geometrical shapes.

Five: Draw polygons using freehand, or approximate divisions of the circle (for the latter see explanation in *Drawing Geometry* by Jon Allen).

Literacy

Four/Five: Control handwriting using an ink pen

Four/Five: Read confidently and independently, (e.g., is able to use appropriate textbooks for an animal project), the majority of the class read with pleasure.

Four/Five: Recognise and indicate punctuation, including direct speech, etc., in reading aloud.

Four: Make reasonable guess at meaning of unknown word from context.

Four: Make accurate written accounts of outings, stories heard as part of the lesson, etc.

Four: Know major parts of speech (noun, pronoun, adjective, verb, adverb, article, preposition, conjunction, interjection).

Four: Set out a formal 'business' letter as compared to informal letter writing ('thank you' letters in Class Three or earlier).

Five: Use dictionary to find unknown words both for spelling and meaning.

Five: Retell story accurately from the point of view of a particular

Four/Five: character (drama) and turn this into reported speech.

Four/Five: Use punctuation marks in free writing; full stops and capitals, commas, quotation marks, exclamation and question marks, the colon for lists and use paragraphs.

Four/Five: Know the use of simple and continuous verb forms in all tenses.

Five: Use syllabification for spelling and to recognise 'key components' (e.g., 'co-respond' in correspondence, etc.)

Five: Use word history to help understand irregular spelling (with help of foreign language teacher, e.g., schwert – a sword).

Five: Identify homophones and homographs (latter to help introduce emphasis).

Five: Make correct use (also for spelling) of the most familiar prefixes and suffixes.

Other skills

The general knowledge points below are not intended to be definitive. These are indications arising out of local/national geography, man, and animal or botany that can give children a sense of knowing the world and thus increasingly making it their own.

Three–Four: Be able to spend night out with class.

Four/Five: Know by heart names of major local/national rivers and in the case of the local river, the tributaries

Four: Know local place names and what they mean (an opportunity for poetry perhaps?)

Five: Know county names.

Five: Recognise flags of St George, St Andrew, St David and the Union flag.

Five: Know ports, centres of industry, airports, etc.

Five: Identify own town and major cities, etc., on U.K. map (develop to Europe and other continents during next years).

Four: Identify common birds, local animals, butterflies, etc.

Four/Five: Identify roots, bulbs, tubers, corms, edible parts of plants, etc.

Five: Sight read simple music (quavers, crochets, minims, semi-breves) in range on one octave plus. Also simple sight singing.

Five: Improvise accompaniment for a well known song (rhythm).

Four: Hold a part in round singing with sensitivity for the whole.

Four: Recognise tonic or 'ground note' of simple major melody by ear.

Four/Five: Identify points of the compass from the position of the sun with reasonable accuracy.

Five: Be aware of lunar phases at a given time.

Five: Use combinations of colours including variations of brown.

Five: Make illustrative paintings from colour. Use light and shade in illustration and painting going towards intensity (colour) perspective.

Four: Be accurate in fine work for paper folding, cutting.

Five: Plan and follow through range of self-selected craft activities.

Five: Work from a design or pre-prepared plan.

Four/Five: Model characteristic forms of animals and birds, certain plant forms (especially fungi, lichen) using wax and/or clay.

11.

Classes Six and Seven checklists

The checklists for Classes Six and Seven could be much more extensive, except they might then appear even more daunting. Many of these will require ongoing practice and amplification into the upper school. The suggestion that assessment is made in Class Seven comes because this allows renditions of shortcomings to be made during the final year, which is fundamentally an opportunity to consolidate, take stock and celebrate with the students the achievements of the previous year. By Class Seven the children will either be confident in the following – or possess the skills that lead towards what is necessary for Class Eight.

Numeracy

Five/Six:	Apply all four rules to fractions including mixed operations (vulgar and mixed numbers).
Five/Six:	Convert fractions to decimals, percentages, and vice versa.
Five/Six:	Estimate results prior to accurate calculation.
Five/Six:	Be able to apply 'speed maths' and short-cut methods appropriately.
Six:	Know powers of numbers.
Seven/Eight:	Approximate square roots.

Six:	Read balance sheets (e.g., bookkeeping for a class outing) and use other 'business' maths, (e.g., profit and loss, discounts, commission, VAT, etc.)
Six:	Work out averages including speed.
Six/Seven:	Make time and speed calculations.
Six:	Work out ratio and scale.
Five–Eight:	Present information via pictograms, pie charts, bar graphs, linear graphs.
Five/Six:	Read co-ordinates (e.g., for map reading).
Six:	Work out simple and compound interest (taxation, etc.).
Seven:	Use negative and positive integers.

Geometry

Six:	Use algebra for general solutions to specific problems.
Six:	Apply principle of substitution.
Six:	Make precise use of compass, ruler, set squares, protractor, dividers, other geometrical instruments.
Six/Seven:	Know theorem of Pythagoras (and its applications).
Seven:	Know properties of triangles, parallel.

Seven: Know and apply formulae for area of regular geometrical forms, including triangle, parallelogram, derivation of π (from approximation $\pi = 3$ radii to approximation of proportion via inductive process). Irregular forms.

Six/Seven: Construct major regular geometric figures.

Literacy

Six: Be able to read books in a range of styles, make use of reference material for study topics and give a verbal or written summary of the main content.

Six: Use precise note-taking skills leading to notes from spoken exposition (avoid during Morning-Lesson exposition. See Appendix L).

Seven: Write in different styles as appropriate, for example, narrative, descriptive, lyrical/atmospheric, informative (i.e. describe the appearance of a fountain pen, explain how it works; tell the story of the pen from its manufacture to being owned by someone; write a piece showing the mood of someone sitting down to write an important letter).

Seven: Use an etymological dictionary (history of words, e.g., Latin and Greek roots) and a thesaurus.

Seven: Use simile, metaphor, hyperbole in connection with the style of the piece.

Six: Identify subject, object and predicate.

Five/Six: Use active and passive voice (and pay attention to the grammar of these).

Seven: Use all punctuation including semi-colon (and 'irregular' punctuation such as the dash).

Six: Use apostrophe for contraction and for possession.

Seven/Eight: Punctuate, and use appropriately, subordinate clauses, relative clauses, clauses of comparison and concession, nouns in apposition[11] (N.B. The point here is not so much to be able to name or even recognise the different clauses as to be able to recognise the main verb of any sentence).

Six: Make a short oral presentation on a given theme from brief notes, for example, a Renaissance figure during a history block or description of a geographical feature, etc.

Six: Show sense of style, for example, in retelling event from different points of view, or according to contrasting moods. Spoken and written.

Six/Seven: Show a sense for metre in verse and be able to imitate simple poetic styles, e.g., ballads (aesthetics of this in Class Eight).

Other skills

Six: Use wide range of reference material and organise information to give a presentation or write an essay.

Seven: Have a feeling for historical sequence. Picture events in British history (appreciate jokes of the '1066 and all that' type).

Five/Six: Show a sense of chronological sequence ('step back' through the generations: What were the roads like? What forms of transport? What clothes were worn and foods eaten?)

Six: Be able to make clear observations of phenomena and describe them accurately (spoken and in writing).

Six: Be able to use an atlas as a resource/ reference book.

Six: Be able to hold a part in playing or singing of compositions for two voices or more.

Six: Sight read music with reasonable accuracy and cope with rests, changes of time signature, accidentals, etc.

Six: Model forms accurately from a thought rather than concrete example.

Seven: Convey observations through illustration.

Six/Seven: Show awareness of heavenly bodies: be able to distinguish stars and planets; pick out major constellations (Plough, North Star, Orion); phases of the moon and its position, understand solstice, equinox, etc.

Seven: Recognise cloud types (could be studied phenomenologically in connection with exploration and discovery leading to meteorology proper in Class Eight).

Seven: Use a wide range of drawing and writing techniques appropriate to purpose or context.

Seven: Plan and execute a complex project in craft using a wide variety of materials.

Movement skills

These should not be neglected after the lower classes but should be developed to increase overall co-ordination and grace. For example, independence of left and right, above and below (such as stepping a dactylic rhythm while clapping anapaests). This is a good time for 'outward-bound' type activities especially where co-operation is encouraged or where the pupils are helped to overcome certain barriers in themselves (heights or enclosed spaces for example). Many schools have found that the Rua Fiola Exploration Island Centre is ideal for the needs of classes at this stage (but beware, a trip such as this needs planning and it is probably wise to establish a class fund very early on for this).

Part II

The Curriculum

12.

Planning ahead

Everyone has a different set of circumstances to support them, or to contend with, in trying to become a Waldorf teacher. Although this handbook is mostly concerned with questions about outer relations, it is at this point that something of the inner relation of the teacher to the work must at least be touched upon. Without this, matters of personal situation become simply questions of lifestyle and that would be much the same as reading the checklists as a series of attainment targets to be 'ticked off' in turn. The spiritual content of the curriculum can become a kind of spiritual luxury unless taken with the wholesome frugality of exercises in self-knowledge. After all, it is not what the teacher *knows* that educates the child, but what the teacher *is* and what the teacher strives to become. That which is developing in a child thus has something to reach for in what the child experiences unconsciously of the teacher's maturation.

How often a small decision with regard to one's private habits has a transforming influence on work in the classroom. When we suffer from inner agitation – or are distracted from the task of teaching – a sort of nervousness enters the class that can be difficult, even impossible, to counter.

Fortunately, the means to rescue the situation, or prevent it from occurring, are always to hand: rhythm, art and preparation.

The rhythm of the year can become a support for our work. During the summer, when term has ended and the pressures are reduced, is probably the only opportunity the teacher has to consider the whole of the coming year. The height of summer enables us to examine the prospect, and we can begin to dip into those lesser-known regions. Background reading can be done in a leisurely way and it is possible to make a map to guide you through the coming terms. However, the most important thing is to *enjoy* the prospect.

It is helpful to choose Morning Lesson themes in connection with the cycle of the year and the seasons, particularly in the younger classes, but this should not be forgotten later on. Themes such as: what part of the year supports the dramatic mythology of the Norsemen; when the phenomena of colour and heat are most evident; which themes are more reflective and which have a more outgoing, active quality that can serve to form an objective plan for the year. It is more effective to use these themes than to leave a less-favoured subject to slip into unconsciousness until the end of the summer term. As with the Morning Lesson itself, the rhythm of the year's work will need balance and contrast, an in-breathing and out-breathing, if the children are not to suffer from sluggishness or inflexibility of soul.

There always seems so much to do, and one of the chief dangers for the teacher is to become so much a doer that the forces needed for teaching become exhausted. To actively set time aside for oneself – to paint, or to make music not directly connected to the class one is teaching – is indispensable and although no one can be constantly productive and creative, one can always find time to read poetry, listen to or play music, or view a painting.

Walking, too, is a sometimes overlooked as a method of relaxation. A walk to school in the morning can provide all the possibilities needed to really *do* the exercises described, for example, in Steiner's *Practical Training in Thinking*. You do not have to live in an area of great natural beauty to observe the changing pattern of clouds or the unfolding of buds on a neighbour's cherry tree. No wonder Rudolf Steiner emphasised the importance of a pre-school walk for the teacher, and if all cars could deliver their occupants a mile from school what a difference that might make to the start of Morning Lesson.

It is said that a Shah once asked a Sufi master what he should do to rule wisely; he received the reply: 'Sleep as long as you can'. That wasn't the answer to suit a potentate but 'sleep enough' is probably the best advice for a Waldorf teacher, especially in the spring term when everyone's strength is at a low ebb and meetings seem to get longer and longer. The most important sleeping time is that before midnight. For most people, one night of shortened sleep will need three to compensate. To ignore such needs is to undermine

the one resource that a Waldorf school needs most, and often the only one it can boast of: the creative energy of its teachers.

Another method to help consolidate strength is the reverse review exercise (Rückshau). Rudolf Steiner gave this exercise as a means of helping to bring order into our life body and thus give it refreshment. It can become the basis for looking back on our teaching in the evening, *provided it is done without passing judgement*, on ourselves or on others as well as at the end of the day. Reviewing our meetings in this way can also be a revelation.

Our colleagues are as much part of the warp and weft of relationships that build the reality of a school as the children we teach. Colleagues too deserve, and need, to be held from time to time in the light of meditative attention before sleep. Confidence in one another has to be built painstakingly and by all concerned. A tendency to form cliques and to gossip behind the backs of colleagues undermines this, and distorts the ability to meet one another in such a way where each could learn from the other and discover what the other has to give.

Our pedagogical meetings could become more productive if the focus was placed practically on the professional development of the teaching group. Such meetings would serve as a stimulus and opportunity for self-development (in this context that means self-development as a teacher). For example, to actively take up and share experiences of working with some of the fundamental anthroposophical exercises, or to allow ten minutes at the beginning of each meeting for the sharing of an imaginative image used in our classroom work, we might achieve much in creating and nurturing the community that is the true heart of the Waldorf school (see *Towards the Deepening of Waldorf*

Education and *Republican Academies*). In this way we might move nearer to a situation where meetings could be seen as part of each teacher's preparation rather than an obstacle to it. Such exercises refresh the soul and help to ensure that the teacher remains inwardly healthy, and that they are thus able to fulfil the four 'qualifications' that Rudolf Steiner set for the teachers of the first Waldorf School (*Discussions with Teachers*).[12]

Progressing through the curriculum

The vital concept is the movement from the whole to the parts. We begin with the whole word, *then* discover what it begins with and what the other sounds are (analysis). The quality of number, the universe of a particular number, leads us to discover the systems and constellations within it. The fairy tale is a world in which art, science and religion remain interconnected. Gradually during Classes Two and Three these start to become distinct and articulated. The unity of the world begins to show that it has different faces and moods. Inside and outside become more clearly differentiated. Now is the time to notice how a variety of types and skills co-operate to form a whole that is a picture of the ideal human community.

Simultaneously we progress from teaching the children to work together and join in, to their being able to participate as distinct individuals, each with a particular part (from unison to rounds). Competition has its place here, though it is not the cunning sort where one intellect is pitted covertly against another, but rather the children testing their whole being, strength, speed and skill against the group, so identifying their unique individuality. (For example, the clash of Agamemnon and Achilles; Achilles sulking in his tent, indicates the negative side of this). Games provide the best, but not the only, medium for this (Rudolf Kischnick games, the Olympics).[13]

The first three classes can be characterised as working with residual imitation while preparing for the more individualised character of the years beyond the ninth-year Rubicon. Classes Four to Six might be characterised as the years of 'self-possession'; the individual gradually absorbs what flows from the class group (the tribe) that the teacher has tried to build up during the previous phase (Norsemen, Greeks and Romans). Thus it is really through Classes Six, Seven and Eight that the circle is broken and differentiation is accomplished.

Below is a summary of this in relation to the curriculum:

From the seventh year

Period of development from infantile thinking – 'realistic unreality' of a self-contained world of thought-images. Memory can now be called on as a transformative process (three-day digestion).

From the ninth year

Transformation of *feeling*. The protection of the imaginative world is ruptured and criticism awakens. Separateness. Need to see authority of teacher under higher authority. Growth at this stage is mainly filling out.

From the twelfth year

Development of *will*. Pubescence. Agility of younger child begins to change. Movement is less rhythmical. Girls mature earlier – tiredness with onset of menstruation. Boys, often more boisterous, express a need for games, etc., growth is mainly lengthening.

Curriculum and basic skills

The 'horizontal' curricula outlined in the following chapters are intended as a possible way to describe the general contents in terms of basic skills. In order to make the presentation complete, I have in each case shown the broad (even lofty) aims that might be taken for the curriculum subject first, then gone on to indicate the more specific objectives and a few of the necessary skills in sequence. These indications remain at the level of learning objectives: for a lesson plan they will need breaking down into smaller steps as learning outcomes (or 'LOUTS') None of the following are definitive in scope or content; they are merely intended to assist teachers in finding their own way to articulate what they plan to do with their classes and according to their own vision and insight. The background reading is given to direct the reader to some of the places where Steiner speaks of the principles for this particular subject and its teaching.

N.B. The following are not year plans. The aim is to help to indicate the development of skills through Morning Lesson blocks. Each teacher gives the breath of life to the dry bones of the themes suggested here. A clear intention can assist in finding the inspiration needed – or at least to give it direction. Aims, skills and lists develop from what is general to what is more particular.. They are intended to provide a basis for planning and record keeping (see Appendix G: Planners and record sheets).

13

Class One
curriculum and basic skills

Morning Lesson: Form drawing[14]

Themes

* Straight and curved
* Form as a basis for writing
* Symmetrical form and form completion

Aims, objectives and skills

* To explore in two-dimensional space the form principles underlying incarnation, 'cosmic' (curve) and 'earthly' (straight line) polarity, and the vortex (spiral) resolving the tension between these.
* To develop vocabulary founded on the sculptural quality of the human form.
* To introduce the drawing of forms in space with the whole body, hand and eye to stimulate spatial orientation (eye tracking, etc.).
* To produce clear linear designs to exercise sense of movement and balance.

* To encourage a sense for form completion and symmetry.
* To draw continuous patterns and sequences introduced later to prepare for cursive writing.

Background reading: *Practical Advice* lecture 1; *Kingdom of Childhood* lecture 4; *A Modern Art of Education* lecture 9.

Morning Lesson: Stories/literacy

Themes

* Traditional fairy stories
* From letter pictures to writing
* Consonants and vowels

Aims, objectives and skills

* To provide a means of connection of inner and outer worlds and *vice versa* via the archetypal images of fairy tales and conversely by raising events in the natural

world towards their imaginative meaning (nature stories).

* To foster kinship with the natural world and a feeling of reverence.
* To help children with individual/social needs.

Morning Lesson: Understanding the natural environment

Themes

* Nature stories (especially weather, minerals, plants, etc.), including stories for seasons or festivals and stories with (non-blatant) pedagogical pictures.
* Stories introducing 'scientific themes' through wonder and reverence for observable phenomena.
* Developing oral skills through telling and retelling of stories and little improvisations based on such retelling.
* Developing illustrative vocabulary, e.g. house, human figure, tree, horse, etc.
* Use of block crayons for 'painting and drawing' and sticks for linear tasks.
* Modelling forms arising from stories (wax or plasticine).
* The imaginative alphabet (not necessarily every letter) uncovered to reveal the abstract letter and associated sound(s).
* Vowels as sounds of soul mood and music
* Introducing Roman capitals (and possibly printed form).
* Developing reading from writing of (at first) known texts (poems, songs, etc.).

* 'Analysis' of sentences to discover individual words, sounds, blends, digraphs, etc.
* Sight vocabulary for reading/spelling as foundation for phonics (own name, days of the week, commonly used words).

N.B. These lessons are the basis for, for example, Local environment in Class Four and much of the geography and some science in later classes.

Aims, objectives and skills

* To encourage a sense of reverence and wonder towards the environment.
* To provide narratives that can help form and sustain 'imaginative participation' with the natural world.
* Objectives and skills as for Stories/literacy.

Background reading: *Practical Advice* lectures 1, 2 and 5; *Soul Economy and Waldorf Education* lecture 9; *Discussions* 3 and 4; *A Modern Art* lecture 8; *Interpretation of Fairy Tales*; *The Renewal of Education* lecture 10.

Recitation of poetry should aim to develop clear flexible speech (no droning) and for this purpose good poetry should be used even if the outer meaning may seem complex. Doggerel only encourages a slovenly use of language (the rule of the cliché) and is unlikely to challenge the children's vocabulary or linguistic competence. Well-formed gesture will help to establish the sense of the verse provided it is in keeping with its movement and rhythm. At the end of Class One (or before) individual verses may be found, preferably written, for each child (see Heinz Müller's *Report Verses in Rudolf Steiner's Art of Education*, Floris Books).

Morning Lesson: Number

Themes

* Quality of numbers from integral unit to diversity
* Pattern and form – related to numerical qualities
* Rhythmic counting and counting patterns
* Number bonds and tables
* 'Personality' of four processes

Aims, objectives and skills

* To work from the whole to the parts.
* To develop sense of oneness, twoness and find examples in the childrens' experience. N.B. a feeling (aesthetic) inner picture for number provides an entry to the quantitative (cardinal) and sequential (ordinal) aspects.
* To establish one-to-one correspondence.
* To introduce quantification via introduction of numbers on their fingers, Roman numerals and/or tallying.
* To encourage clear writing of Arabic numerals (and associated quantities).
* To teach counting sequences to 100 (writing of higher numbers).
* To teach counting in 2s, 3s, 5s, 10s.
* To introduce multiplication of above tables through rhythmic movement, clapping, etc.
* To memorise number bonds to 20.
* To use all the above for mental arithmetic.
* To provide experiences (mainly narrative) of the four rules through practical activity with quantities including the class itself.
* To introduce pictorial record of 'sums' leading to the writing of them.
* To introduce character of plus, minus, multiply, divide (with signs).
* To apply form drawing to number patterns.

Background reading: *Theory of Knowledge*, end of Chapter 12; *A Modern Art* lecture 9; *Discussions* 4; *Kingdom of Childhood* lecture 5.

Non-Morning Lesson

* Two contrasting foreign languages (frequently French and German – but this will depend upon school policy).
* Handwork and crafts (including, but not exclusively, knitting/sewing).
* Plenty of exploration of artistic subjects as a foundation for future learning.
* Plenty of opportunity to develop movement skills.
* Religion may start here or in Class Two depending on the policy of the school.
* Walks with a purpose.

14.

Class Two
curriculum and basic skills

Morning Lesson: Form drawing

This may appear more frequently as an extra lesson or as a part of another Morning Lesson block during Class Two (as before).

Background reading: *Discussions* 3 pp 38–39.

Themes

* Symmetry and reflections
* Sequences of form in transformation
* Borders for Morning Lesson books
* Running and rhythmical forms

Aims, objectives and skills

* Development and consolidation of skills introduced in Class One.
* Practise in rhythmic drawing to prepare for cursive writing.
* Dynamic imagination, e.g., in changing curved line form to varied straight line form, to curves, and similarly in creating sequences (metamorphosis).
* Developing surer and freer use of drawing materials and increasing rhythmicity.

Morning Lesson: Literature and language

Background Reading: *Discussions 4* (important section of fables); also beginning of *5* and *6*; *Kingdom of Childhood* lecture 4.

Themes

* Some fairy tales not appropriate for Class One
* Fables
* Legends of the Saints
* Nature stories, especially concerning the animal world
* Understanding the local environment
* Pedagogical stories

Aims, objectives and skills

* To give a picture of the striving of the human being in respect to the ideal (saints) and to morality in earthly action and impulses (fables).
* To introduce the morality of the fable – the moral should, of course, remain implicit and not be given, as it is in most printed versions (see background reading, *Discussions with Teachers*).
* To encourage reverence for that in humanity which aspires towards the Divine and confidence in the natural order.
* To enable transition from capital letters to upper and lower case cursive script.
* To develop the retelling/improvisation of stories of the children's creation and writing of short fables based on these (help with vocabulary will be needed). (N.B. In improvisation 'characterisation' of animals, for example, can now be expected to be inwardly precise).
* To provide opportunities for assignments such as the retelling of simple events from class experience – this should be possible towards the end of this class.
* To teach phonic skills (especially long and short vowels, final 'e', etc.), in order to enable children to accomplish the above. (N.B. in free writing children should be able to make errors without interrupting the flow of thought – 'the way adults spell' can be added later – see *Practical Advice* pp 80–83).
* To introduce the first reading books. The best are ones prepared by the teacher based on stories the children know well (again the brief fable is useful). Reading of stories augments children's reading their own handwriting, the teacher's writing, poetry and songs that they know by heart.
* To engage the class in conversations around the theme of the stories.
* To introduce punctuation through sentence rhythms (breathing) as experienced first in speaking/recitation/reading aloud.

I have omitted mention of descriptive grammar here. In Stockmeyer, Steiner is quoted as indicating a beginning of grammar teaching in Class Two (nouns and verbs with their tenses) and no doubt something can be done at this stage (beginning with movement). However, in *A Modern Art*, p.173–176, Steiner suggests that this should begin during the ninth year (N.B. local differences). Having tried both, and spoken to others who have done so, I feel the latter is the most appropriate approach so far as *explicit* teaching is concerned.

Class Two can provide an excellent opportunity to take nature stories in connection with the quality of the seasons as a separate theme. During Class One the children will have experienced the festivals through class and school celebrations, through the seasonal table, pictures and stories chosen as reflecting their mood. In Class Two this will no doubt continue but can be made more conscious. Themes such as the 'story of the cloud' might suit the period from Easter to Ascension, or stories and legends concerning fruits and grains in autumn. The possibilities are endless. The aim is to bring about an imaginative participation with the rhythm of the year, with the festivals as a focus. In this way the ground is further prepared for practical activities in Class Three and environmental education generally.

Morning Lesson: Arithmetic

Background reading as before.

Themes

* Four rules
* All-important number bonds
* Odd and even numbers
* Place value
* Numerical patterns (based on form patterns of Class One)

Aims, objectives and skills

* To develop understanding for the character of the four rules and use of the symbols (including 'equals'). Children should become secure in the writing of sums.
* To introduce narrative form of mental arithmetic, supplemented by use of a number 'staircase' or 'ladder'.
* To introduce hundreds, tens and units pictorially. Writing higher numbers with distinct columns.
* To teach times tables 1–12 in order, first as multiplication $12 = 3 \times 4$ but also: $3 \times 4 = 12$, $4 \times 3 = 12$ and 'there are three fours in twelve', etc.
* To create large-scale forms to show the patterns of times tables (e.g. a ball of wool or string to create star form of 4 times table).

Non-Morning Lesson

Themes

* Two foreign languages
* Eurythmy
* Handwork/craft
* Painting
* Drawing
* Music
* Modelling
* Games
* Religion

15.

Class Three
curriculum and basic skills

Form drawing

At this stage this is unlikely to be a specific Morning Lesson but appears in connection with others or as an extra lesson.

Themes

* More complex running forms and rhythmic patterns
* Spirals and forms that coil, overlap and intertwine
* Mirrors/reflections
* Four-fold symmetry, including rotational symmetries
* Forms based on triangles, squares, pentagons, etc.

Aims, objectives and skills

* To develop further 'formal imagination', seeing all round a form, including forms with an element of crossover.
* To study fundamental elements of design, balance, coherence and contrast.

* To encourage the application of this to handwork (e.g. embroidery).
* To explore lettering for specific purposes (e.g. title pages).

Morning Lesson: Literature and literacy

Themes

* Old Testament, from Creation and the Fall to Noah, Abraham, Moses, Samuel, Saul, David and Solomon
* Specific stories for festivals, e.g. Tobias and the Angel or Jonah (Easter), Elijah (midsummer)
* Tales related to farming, building and the crafts

N.B. *Literature* is not a religion lesson. Steiner speaks of this theme as being the study of 'classical literature alongside other classical literature'.

Aims, objectives and skills

* To prepare the child's feeling-life for a recognition of the Divine both within human struggling and separate from it.
* To introduce stories that underpin many literary cultural references and the general development of Western thought.
* To continue to develop clear narrative sentences through 'free' retelling of parts of stories.
* To show how building of sentences corresponds to the process of house-building: nouns as materials, verbs as the builders...
* To introduce more awareness into the child's experience of language through grammar, e.g. showing nouns through Adam naming the animals, verbs through what the animals do.
* To modulate verbs from this – adjectives and adverbs.
* To introduce an appropriate use of incantation in recitation, e.g. speaking of psalms or other passages from the Old Testament.
* To encourage conscious use of comma (as a breathing space), full stop, exclamation mark and question mark.
* To provide topics for illustration involving dramatic contrast – use of colour to support this.
* To stimulate development from class readers to individual readers for a majority of the class.

Background reading: *Temple Legend* Lecture 2; *Genesis* (Munich 1910).

Morning Lesson: Practical activities

This is the first technology lesson.

Themes

* Archetypal technology – farming, husbandry, crafts, house-building, etc.
* The co-operation of human beings to provide what is needful to one another
* Understanding that everything technical or manufactured is ultimately derived from nature

Aims, objectives and skills

* To continue on from the work of nature and home environment stories of Classes One and Two and carry these into the realm where the human being intervenes to help or hinder. (Theme is present in Old Testament stories too.)
* To help to develop a sense of processes at work in which humanity can achieve, and the dependence of this on natural processes.
* To provide pictures of archetypal human activities (e.g. the fisherman travels over the waters of the unconscious to draw life forces from thence to consciousness or the land, the blacksmith wields the element of fire in order to stamp human thinking onto the physical through the power of will, the shepherd humanises aspects of the animal world through tending the needs of the flock).

* To encourage co-operation in the class group through individuals bringing their abilities together to realise a project.
* To develop dexterity in the use of materials, thus leading to devotion in their handling.
* To encourage the writing of clear concise descriptions of processes that the children have experienced.
* To introduce appropriate 'manners' in visiting farms, craftsman, etc.
* To stimulate the writing of 'thank you' letters and letters of enquiry.[15]
* To prepare for local history and geography in Class Four by providing insight into the human activities that have shaped these.
* To encourage expressive illustration of objective processes.
* To provide opportunity to explore planning and making of models of houses, etc.
* To enable practical study of milking, bricklaying, carding, spinning, weaving, felting, bread making, butter making, etc.
* To engage the children in the sketching of 'plans'.

Background reading: *Lectures to Teachers* Lecture 10 (the Dornach Christmas Course 1921–22).

Morning Lesson: Mathematics

Exploring the application of number work to practical measure; link with practical activity blocks.

Themes

* From body measures to standard units (decision has to be made whether to teach imperial only or metric as well; while feet and inches are still commonplace some units may be regarded as redundant)
* Measures of weights and liquids
* Time, money calculations, especially in connection with quantities, markets/shops
* 'Long' multiplication and division with remainders – to be followed up in the following year

Aims, objectives and skills

* To show the human being as the origin of measure.
* To lead from quality of number to quantity, but qualities remain evident in commutativity (correspondence of processes and factors).
* To introduce sequential thinking (spatial quality).
* To provide opportunities for estimation before measurement (particularly in terms of body measures, e.g. six of my paces to reach the door in a straight line, or my height once and once more to reach the branch of that tree).
* To give a wide experience of measurement using a variety of units.
* To introduce work with different number bases via imperial measures (implicit).
* To introduce standard metric measures as whole units, especially centimetres, metres, kilometres, litres, kilograms, etc. (N.B. at this stage 1m 53cm, not 1.53m).
* To teach reading of time, analogue then digital.

* To introduce area calculation in connection with practical activities, e.g. size of rooms in a house being planned (N.B. Use of money presents first glimpse of the decimal system – prepare for Class Five).
* Helping to plan ahead using the first most immediate and human means, e.g., organising page layout using fingers or spans.

Non-Morning Lesson

Recommendations are the same as for Class Two.

Visits to building sites and farms – these will need a great deal of organisation and preparation (e.g. safety issues for farm visits can be stringent and *risk assessments should be drawn up*).

In combined-class schools it is worth considering the introduction of certain 'linking' topics in Classes Three to Four as later there is less opportunity to do so. For example, a Morning Lesson theme that explores other basic (helping) services such as the fire brigade, post or rail might be introduced. A hybrid Morning Lesson with a theme such as 'Homes and habitat' might link house-building and human and animal/zoology. Such a lesson could take the form of a study of human habitations e.g. Bedouin, Native American and Inuit. Alongside these a teacher might introduce a comparison with animal nests and shelters.

16.

A selection of lessons from the curriculum for Classes Four to Eight

What follows is a sample of some of the Morning Lessons for Classes Four to Eight. Obviously the selection is not comprehensive, but I have sought to cover the main types of lessons. However, it must be understood that each Morning Lesson has its own aims and objectives, those for one science subject may occur for another, but each has its own specific tone and trend.

Morning Lesson: Arithmetic

Class Four. Two or three morning lessons

N.B. The list of 'Aims, objectives and skills' indicated for subjects where **more than one** Morning Lesson block is envisaged should be divided among each of the blocks; overarching 'aims' may well apply to the whole series, however.

Themes

* Fractions from whole to the parts, at first pictorially (sometimes known as halving your cake and eating it) then through number patterns and as pure number relationship. The fracturing of the whole will be balanced through the discovery of the number relationships that connect seemingly different worlds (halves, thirds, quarters, fifths, etc.) with one another.

* Factors and further work with square numbers (e.g. Eratosthenes' sieve) leading to study of perfect, deficient, abundant and prime numbers. Lowest common multiple, highest common factor, lowest common denominator, multiplication (first as indicated by the word 'of', 'half of 8 is 4', 'half of a third is one sixth', etc.) addition and subtraction. Division of fractions might be introduced in the form: 'how many halves in 7', 'how many quarters in a half' (the method, i.e. 'turn the second fraction, the divisor, upside down and multiply', might be introduced in Class Five).

* Elaboration of all previous mathematical work relevant to this.

* Include further work in measurement and fractions of measures.

Aims, objectives and skills

* To provide a sense for how the material world breaks down into particles, the realm of life extends beyond this, the rhythmic patterns of numbers reassembles 'atomic and sub-atomic' physicality.
* To show the lawfulness of numerical relationships.
* To lead from concrete operations, to pictorial representation of fractions, to an appreciation of the purely numerical (abstract) appreciation of the subject.
* To work with fractions in order to reinforce what has been achieved so far by way of number (principally multiplication) patterns and mathematics in general, e.g. the indispensability of time tables (this is a good time to introduce and explore time-tables square), the connection with number bases related to imperial measures (e.g. one foot is one-third of a yard) and reading analogue time, etc. It also builds a bridge from the concrete to abstract.
* To encourage flexibility in thinking about a phenomenon (in this case fractions) from different points of view, e.g., a half is 2 quarters, 4 eighths, etc. but also 3 sixths, 7 fourteenths…
* To bring the class to a point where they feel 'fractions are easy' (at least in principle); the more able children should feel the excitement of number combinations and their beauty.
* To explore expansion and simplification of fractions.
* To learn and be able to use the algorithms for the calculation of fraction problems.

* To introduce calculation of fractions of whole numbers and other fractions (multiplying).
* To teach addition and subtraction of fractions.
* To introduce vulgar fractions, mixed numbers and improper fractions.
* To familiarise the class with the specialised vocabulary of mathematics relevant to this subject area – factor, denominator, numerator, etc. (the beginnings of a mathematical dictionary, simple etymology, spelling).
* To introduce 'Fraction drawings' – geometrical form drawing involving patterns deriving from freehand division of circle, exact freehand drawing of other geometrical shapes and divisions of them.

Development

Decimal fractions, ratio, percentages, mensuration, even 'substitution' for solving algebraic equations could be traced back to the operations that are learned in manipulating fractions.

Background reading: *The Kingdom of Childhood*, lecture 7 (Torquay 1924); the *Basel Course* (14 lectures, May 1920); *A Modern Art of Education* lecture 9.

N.B. At this stage at least two practice lessons per week will be needed for this subject to continue the consolidation of all previous work.

Morning Lesson: Human and animal

Classes Four and Five zoology. Two Morning Lessons, one each year – insects and other animals closely associated with plants might be studied in connection with botany in Class Six.

Themes

* Threefold nature of the human form
* Morphology, correspondence between specialised forms of animals and human systems (Class Four) and soul characteristics and qualities (Class Five)
* Human form is incomplete, animal forms more perfectly adapted to particular situations
* Animal specialisms related to and arising out of their habitat
* Environmental conservation and biodiversity, the biography of a species (particularly in Class Five)
* Temperamental qualities of animal types (Class Five), e.g. the choleric wolverine, phlegmatic sloth, melancholic camel and sanguine prairie dog
* Exploring animal groups (Class Five)

Aims, objectives and skills

* To show how moral choice is related to the potential of the human hand; human freedom to utilise the upper limbs, especially by serving others and the environment in which she or he is placed, and not simply one's own needs.

* To engender respect and sympathy for the animal world.
* To show how technology arises from the comparative vulnerability and incomplete development of humankind.
* To explore the animal and environmental 'gesture' through drawing and painting; using colour impressionistically.
* To write precise characterisations of the animals studied (the beginnings of scientific description).
* To write more impressionistic pieces from another (the animal's) point of view.
* To write animal 'fables' or 'Just So'-type stories.
* To model characteristic animal forms in clay.
* To provide individualised topics in the form of short studies (e.g.: a domestic animal, native fauna, studies of a specific species).

N.B. In Class Six, the teaching of zoology might feature as part of a second botany block. The study of geographical regions also allows for work on the animals inhabiting specific types of environment).

Background reading: *Foundations of Human Experience (Study of Man)* lectures 4 and 12; *Practical Advice* Lecture 7; *Discussions with Teachers* sessions 9-11; *Soul Economy* lecture 10.

Morning Lesson: History

Class Five. Usually two morning lessons.

Themes

* The emergence of history from mythology and legend – key pictures.

* The evolution of human consciousness as indicated by the development of cultures from the Indo-European migration (partly reflected in the Upanishads and the Rigvedas) to the rise and fall of Classical and Alexandrian Greece.
* This development seen as a gradual coming to terms with, and increasing ability of, human beings to manipulate or control their environment. Alongside this, mythological consciousness changes from a sense of an intimate omnipresence of spiritual beings to one where the gods look on, intervening as outside agents in human lives. For example, Pre-Vedic India – the myth of Manu; Avestan culture (the first, ancient agrarian 'revolution'); from Ra to Isis and Osirus and Horus (ancient Egypt); Sumerian to Assyrian Mesopotamia depicted in the epic of Gilgamesh; Homeric, Classical and Alexandrian Greece.
* A similar development could be traced in a single country, in particular, ancient China or Japan (these could also form part of a later geography lesson block).
* Significant images from the periods studied – planar, rather than linear history.

Aims, objectives and skills

* To indicate the continuity of human cultural development, demonstrating that human consciousness and institutions evolve.
* To awaken interest in the drama of history and convey the interaction of human beings and their environment over time.
* To provide a context for the understanding of the present.
* In particular to provide the class with connection between some of the cultural reference points of western civilisation and the ancient mythologies or traditions from which these arose.
* To explore the interaction of individuals and communities, especially through biographies of legendary and historical personalities.
* To explore the motifs and designs typical of the ancient cultures for which we have records.
* To encourage the creative use of these for the presentation of work in the Morning Lesson book, including an exploration of fonts and lettering using the forms of ancient scripts.
* To explore hieroglyphs and icons.
* To learn poetry, music or other arts relevant to this, possibly including some Greek recitation, the hexameter, etc.
* To make a practical and artistic study of the development of writing from prehistoric, oral cultures, to the ancient, historical, societies.
* To introduce the etymology of English words originating from Sanskrit, Greek, etc. Spelling patterns distinctive to these, e.g. 'ph', 'kh', words ending with 'ah', etc. How these words such as 'physics', 'veranda', 'bungalow' came into English.
* To explore modern versions of ancient names – using examples from among the class.
* To introduce 'philosophy' via 'thumbnail sketches' of thinkers associated with the 'discovery of logic' – Solon, Thales, Pythagoras, Socrates and Plato, Aristotle, etc.
* To introduce the use of the semicolon and colon in sentence structure for the principle of parallel construction (characteristic

of the way Greek thought was frequently expressed), e.g. 'Best of all things is water; but gold, like gleaming fire/ by night outshines all pride of wealth beside' (*Olympia 1*, Pindar); or: 'But his command is plain: the parricide must be destroyed' (*Oedipus the King*, Sophocles).

Background reading: *Practical Advice* lectures 8 and 10; *Basel Course* lecture 12; *Discussions with Teachers* 14; *Renewal of Education* lecture 12.

Morning Lesson: Physics

Classes Six and Seven. Two and three blocks over the two years.

Themes

Mainly during Class Six:
* Sound – sources, pitch and volume, creating sounds, transmission of sounds, formative qualities (e.g. the Chladni plate).
* Light – light and darkness, origins of light, nature and properties of colour (looking through the prism), complementaries and the after-image.
* Heat – qualities of warmth and cold, sources of heat, effects of heat and cold.
* Magnetism – properties and materials, the earth's field and the compass, propagation and induction.
* Static electricity – generation of static, detection, properties.

Mainly during Class Seven:
* Sound – musical intervals, resonance,

instrument design, the phonograph and gramophone.
* Light – shadows, reflections and lenses, images (e.g. camera obscura, pinhole camera).
* Heat – measurement.
* Electromagnetism – generation of static and current electricity, relationship of electricity and magnetism.
* Mechanics – maximising effort, basic machines (levers and the fulcrum, pulley, wheel and axle, wedge, inclined plane, screw and gears), formulae for mechanical processes (possibly in mathematics), friction.

Aims, objectives and skills

* To lead from the artistic to the scientific.
* To encourage 'devotion to phenomenon' in the form of precise observation; training in 'paying attention consciously'.
* To provide the children with insights into 'the wonderful' in everyday experience and to engage them in contemplating these things holistically, from perception to thought process.
* To introduce the way affective writing can be informed by scientific perception – stories or plays derived from the phenomena.
* To produce clear expository writing.
* To show the necessity for linear procedures – step-by-step recipes of 'experiments' that can be easily replicated.
* To design charts and tables of results and conclusions.
* To introduce standard laboratory reports that include equipment, method, observation, conclusion.
* To create diagrams as a non- or part-verbal record of experiments observed.

* To explore colour through the painting of colour exercises.
* To engage the class in the way in which experiments are designed.
* To identify similar or identical phenomena in everyday contexts and the application of principles to manufactured objects.
* To introduce specialised words for clear communication; vocabulary, glossaries, spelling.
* To explore the figurative use of such terms in common speech or poetry, etc.
* To provide opportunity for practice of note writing, e.g. essential points from experiments, summaries, etc.

Morning Lesson: English

Class Seven. Three to four weeks writer's workshop, often titled 'Wish, wonder and surprise'.

Themes

* The practical exploration of writing in different moods; in particular, the subtle forms that can be used to express longing or want, admiration and awe, incredulity or shock.
* The craft of writing – choice, arrangement and juxtaposition of words, use of punctuation, types of imagery and linguistic 'tone'
and their potential for communication.
* Appropriate style and 'register'.

Aims, objectives and skills

* To raise to consciousness some of the burgeoning feeling of the young person through the use of language, to provide some means with which to delineate the contours of the soul.
* To indicate the way in which language works on us and in us, both as a means of access and in the form of the potential danger of manipulation, and to raise awareness of the issues involved in this.
* To encourage an informed appreciation of literature in a variety of styles – poetic, narrative, illustrative, explanatory, etc.
* To explore these through the practice of writing and through examples.
* To explore the potential range and nuances of English vocabulary.
* To elicit precise observation and the means to communicate it.
* To write in a range of styles.
* To study imagery and its effect; metaphor and simile.
* To paint 'word pictures', onomatopoeia, assonance, alliteration, etc.
* To consider tall stories and boasts as hyperbole, bathos, irony.
* To write reports, instructions, descriptions in differing styles (e.g. police, newspaper, literary, etc.); 'plain and purple prose'.
* To study imperative, indicative and subjunctive moods (the grammar of these might be better taught as an English lesson prior to the Morning Lesson).
* To study the comparative use of dictionary and thesaurus, the etymological dictionary and its possibilities.

* To introduce the purpose and nature of drafting and redrafting written work, editing and proofreading (members of the class might compile a reference book for some of the essential stylistic rules for clear communication – it's a good idea to show examples of how the best writers break these rules from time to time and the reasons for this, in much the same way that one might look for contrasting views of historical characters or events).
* To study how publishing works.
* To consider the uses and limitations of technology.

N.B. The production of a class anthology from this block might provide practical experience of the three final points. A local publisher, if available, might be asked to make a contribution by explaining the work involved and advise the students on the enterprise. Such a project would provide opportunity to examine types of money (e.g. gift, loan, purchase) and to explore some useful practical skills (e.g. budgeting, how to make a simple business plan, how to use bank services). This would also raise issues such as the problems of debt, what credit and collateral are about, LETS, credit unions, inflation, and even matters such as why certain products are selected for sale and others not, or how and to what end goods that are displayed in the shop might be touched upon. Young people at this stage tend to have high aspirations regarding economics; it's not a bad idea to introduce them to some of the realities too, but the work involved would need to take in a good sized block of non-Morning Lesson time).

Morning Lesson: The human body

Class Eight. One block of four weeks or two of three weeks to study anatomy and development.

Themes

* From birth to the grave, including an overview of the processes involved in conception and birth, maturation (especially childhood to adolescence), blood system, muscles and bones.
* Health education issues connected with the above, pregnancy, contraception, childhood illnesses, immunisation, venereal diseases, and other matters not previously dealt with in the Health, hygiene and nutrition block during Class Seven.
* That death is essential to life (not explicit, but the presence and use for demonstration of a real skeleton brings the question with it into the classroom).
* The question of 'disability', 'differentness', apparent 'abnormality' and 'naturalness' (biographies of the 'elephant man', Christopher Nolan's *Beneath the Eye of the Clock*, some account of 'wolf children', Casper Hauser and others may be helpful). In other words, the question of what makes a human being human.

Aims, objectives and skills

* To encourage a sense of 'educated' wonder and reverence for the design of living forms.
* To provide the class with a sense of confidence in human development; the human being as a process, not a completed fact.
* To bring scientific precision, and delight in the phenomena of humankind, into connection with an artistic appreciation of the human form.
* To bring together many of the themes that will have been touched upon during the previous Morning Lessons (Classes One to Eight).
* To help to encourage recognition that the word 'normal' has a wide range held together by distinctive human qualities shared by all members of humanity.
* To observe one's experience in order to listen to what all the senses and feelings present to one's thinking as material for understanding.
* To elicit exact observation in the modelling and drawing of bones, etc.
* To provide opportunity to learn some medical Latin, showing the pictorial nature of many of the terms – spelling of characteristic Latinate forms.
* To write in a range of styles, with emphasis on clear exposition, theme and variation.

17.

Morning Lessons in theory

The Morning Lesson is to the teacher what the book is to the novelist or the concert performance to the composer. But whereas the reader or listener is often relatively remote from the artist in this analogy, the class and the individual child in it is both the *medium* and *audience* with which the Waldorf teacher works.

The subject matter provides a grammar, an underlying logic, upon which the pedagogical dialogue is sustained and developed. It goes without saying, therefore, that there will be an infinite number of variations as to how the Morning Lesson can be shaped and as many reasons for the particular shape it receives. But, whatever the form, it must work for the children.

The following points are offered to assist teachers in finding an approach that is most apt for their class and circumstances, in accordance with the theme and aim of the lesson in its entirety.

The section on preparation (the three 'Rs') is intended to help with day-to-day readiness. Here we are concerned with points to help find a perspective on the whole sequence of a Morning Lesson, and to consider the rhythm of those precious 120 minutes.

* Where is the lesson going? There needs to be an overall plan that is not set in concrete but focuses very specific intentions. Resist the temptation to plan one day to the next. You need to know what skills you want to help the class develop and what steps need to be taken during the course of the whole Morning Lesson (and school year).

* Try to avoid getting bogged down with some apparently fascinating titbit. For instance, spending a fortnight of a four-week block on Ancient Egypt and Mesopotamia modelling mummies and describing embalming in detail probably gives a distorted picture of the Third Post-Atlantean epoch. Finding the archetype, e.g. in the myth of Isis and Osiris, provides a key to unlock the essential.

* 'One hundred and twenty per cent preparation is needed in order to make use of fifty per cent afterwards' (Lievegoed). The seventy per cent is not wasted, but resonates within the smaller portion the children directly receive.

* The fifty per cent that can be given will need to be treated with economy. The art of characterisation, as Rudolf Steiner called it, is the building of word pictures through which more can be said than meets the eye.

✴ You could call this the magic of teaching. Magic, too, needs scrupulous preparation.

✴ What interested you in researching the subject? That is probably a good starting point.

✴ Part of the economy of teaching, paradoxically enough, is to say the same thing three times without ever repeating what has already been said. At the end of the lesson it is a good idea to remind the class of what they have learned (get them to tell you tomorrow).

✴ Most important of all, whatever you may have prepared, be ready to give it up if it isn't working. But ensure that you have planned what the class will do with what you *do* present and leave sufficient time for them to work independently on this. While they are working, individual coaching can be given and observational notes can be made for your diagnostic record of the class.

Shaping the Morning Lesson

Do first ▼ *Comprehend with feeling* ▼ *Understand*

Willing, feeling and thinking will weave through the lesson if we follow the above routine, for each element is itself threefold. From there we can build something that might look like this:

1. Incarnating exercise, register, Morning Verse.

2. Circle time/feeling-will engagement (Points 1 and 2 should take not more than 30–40 minutes for Classes One to Three, down to 15–20 minutes in Classes Six to Eight.

3. The class takes possession of the previous day's work (recall/retelling/free-rendering/ enacting).

4. New content.

5. Book work, essay writing, etc.

6. Practice time for some element of the lesson (or regular mental arithmetic).

7. An artistic activity related to the lesson theme.

8. Celebration – look at what has been done (completed work from today or previous day).

9. A thought or challenge for tomorrow (includes a reminder of what was covered today).

10. Story (if not at point 4) and close.

1. Incarnating exercise

The incarnating exercise would be very short, a clapping sequence or rhythm, and later on a short concentration exercise to help overcome the fatigue of a car journey to school and to help the children to be fully present. The register also helps to call the 'I' to be present (the ego forms a connection with the full name, so avoid shortenings). In some schools it is the practice to call the child's whole name – first, middle and surname.

2. Circle time

'Circle time' (although this does not always have to be in a circle, especially once children get older) diminishes and becomes more specific from Classes One to Eight (as indicated). This might consist of elements from the following (all related in some way to the Morning Lesson theme).

Classes One to Three would normally begin with Group A, progress to Group B and do a little from Group C, normally culminating with something from Group D (which will include 'birthday verses' if used).

Classes Four to Five would mainly feature items from Group B and Group C with occasional items from Group A culminating in Group D.

Classes Six to Eight would use mainly Group C, culminating in Group D, with a little from Group B and very occasionally from Group A.

N.B. In Classes One to Three one would normally allow 40 minutes for this – maximum – with the time reducing throughout Classes Four to Eight, say 15–20 minutes by Class Eight).

Group A	Group B	Group C	Group D
Ring games	Improvised acting	Instrumental music	Recitation
Skipping	Mime	Concentration exercises	Speech work (including individual report verses)
Stepping	Exercises from Eurythmy lesson*	Quick quizzes related to Morning Lesson (may lead to recall)	Steiner's Speech exercises for children
Clapping	Singing		
	Dancing		

Check with specialist teacher or trained eurythmist

3. Recall time

The recall time should have variety, with an emphasis on giving the class an opportunity to show what has been working in them since the previous day – and to make something of this principle of 'free rendering'. If this is not given room, what one wants to work on from the night becomes a potentially disruptive force today. This part of the lesson relates to the second stage of the 'three-day rhythm'. A common misunderstanding of the three-day rhythm is that the recall inhibits the bringing of a new element ▼, as if nothing new can happen until the process has been completed. Clearly not everything can be worked through in this way, but major teaching points certainly should be.

One way of picturing the process is as a series of overlapping fence lathes, or, better still as the dynamic image comes nearer to the reality, as a series of waves. Each day (with the exception of Monday) would thus include an element of recall (revivifying the content of the previous day), while Wednesday, Thursday and Friday include a third step – that of coming to a conclusion.

See further discussions of new elements overleaf.

Monday	Tuesday	Wednesday	Thursday	Friday
First day (This is a good day on which to give an overview – moon quality)	Second Day	Third Day		
Experience ▼	Judgement	Understanding (concept)	Application	
	New Element ▼	Judgement	Understanding	
		New Element ▼	Judgement	Understanding Sum up the week (something to think about for Monday?)

Elements 4–10

* Presenting a new element may involve a story, characterisation, and practical exercise, making a picture for the class, or any number or combination of these.

* Work in books (e.g. essay writing), recording what has been learned, creating the exercise/text book.

* Practice of some skill learned as a part of the Morning Lesson (from any previous day).

* Illustration, drawing, map-making, modelling, copying an historical portrait, making a pictorial representation of information, etc.

* The teacher will have observed the class at work and given help where needed; there should be a moment to look at what has been done and attention can be drawn to particular points (a moment of celebration).

* This may not be setting homework but it's good for the class to have something to think about, a small task or a question for tomorrow, even if this is not formal homework.

* If a story did not feature as part of the new content, it might appear here (the art of storytelling should figure with other arts, in its own right). A closing verse or a grace is a moment of peace, harmonising the out-breathing.

Observe how the children lead out or prepare for break. This will often give important clues as to how the lesson has worked and especially whether the children have been held on too short a rein or not been engaged deeply enough during the lesson.

Transitions

One of the many grave dangers in setting out a scheme such as the one above is that it has the appearance of nine distinct stages or steps. Thinking divides; but the Morning Lesson is about feeling-willing and feeling-thinking: in short, it is rhythmic. Between systole and diastole is the dynamic process of the heart, not a pause; or what you could call the physiological equivalent of a gap in the market. So the truth is, when we teach well there are *no transitions*. Instead the lemniscate of teacher-learner and learner-teacher adjusts dynamically, and there is no need for elevator music to help fill the time. The teacher needs to draw on and, therefore cultivate, her inner musician. Some lessons may be less good than others, but viewing activities as having 'transitions' between them is not helpful thinking. Waldorf teaching is an organic activity, not prefabricated construction work: there are no transitions, only the swirls and eddies of a flow.

Here are a few suggestions as to how to 'dump the transitions':

* If there are desks to move then that can be a pedagogical game – 'The magician is going to turn around. If he hears a chair clatter or desk squeak, he'll jump round and make anyone moving sit silent as a stone at the front. Can you defeat him today, so that no one has to join him and he doesn't get a chance to jump at all?' Or use something intriguing: 'Tintinnabulation', that's a strange sounding word! When you've moved the chairs, I'll give you four clues so you can find out what it means, but every noise that shows

on my 'decibel reader' will lose you a clue and you may have to find it in a dictionary instead'. Or realistic: 'Have you ever been to a concert and seen how the orchestra warms up? But when the conductor arrives, everyone has to be ready to play! Take out your flutes. The conductor is just getting ready, as soon as she steps up to the podium and raises her hands to conduct, all the instruments are tuned and every player is ready to strike up the overture'.

* The principle of 'Chinese whispers' can also be used so that the children give instructions to one another (but watch out – some children love to see the message go wrong).

* Things need to change – have a song at the ready, preferably with actions of some sort. Simply start singing until everyone joins in. Then try controlled speeding up and slowing down, getting louder, then quieter. Or have a piece of music to play that indicates, 'stand up', 'walk around the room', 'hop', 'skip', 'sit down', etc., all of which are good for aural discrimination. Or try body geography games in which melodies can be used to denote, 'clear away, story time, etc'. Or try 'One, two, three, four, five, six, seven:/ Everybody ready before eleven:/ One, two, three, etc. … / Eleven is a bridge with two long legs, / Down on the riverbank, the tide leaves the dregs'. 'Well done, Semele, well done Polonius… (and so on)… are any washed up? Do any love to crawl? / Dy… no, no one at all!'

* Show a word connected with the subject of the lesson to the class on slate or scrap card – 'Look closely… Watch! You have two minutes. When I say, "now" get everything ready for the next part of the lesson, then write this word (now hidden) in your note books'. Check and correct, ask for different ways to remember such a spelling. Then lead straight into whatever you have to present, including, at some point, the new word that most of the class can now spell.

* Write your instructions on the blackboard and observe the class. Simply announce, 'Ah, Socrates is the first to notice. Well observed' – provided you have the goodwill of the class, the others will soon follow Socrates' lead.

* It helps a great deal, of course, if the class know the lesson rhythm and are anticipating the next activity – but take care not to allow things to become too automatic either.

Some ideas for circles

Some of these can also be used as indicated above. These suggestions are mainly for Classes One to Three (though some can be adapted for Classes Four and Five).

* Ring or circle games – especially those involving going out, or 'turning' the circle, weaving or dissolving and remaking it, and spirals, or games involving opposing lines ('ebb' and 'flow' games), lemniscate forms (this indicates a sequence of development from the classic ring game, and ring and centre games of Kindergarten, some of which may still be appropriate at the beginning of Class One).

* Exercises from *Take Time* by Mary Nash-Wortham and Jean Hunt (Robinswood Press) – beanbags, body geography, aural discrimination. Also *Gesture Games* by Wilma Ellersiek and Connie Manson/Lyn Willwerth.

* Foot exercises and vowels (check with the school eurythmist).
* Form walking and drawing in the air.
* Similar for moving in symmetry and 'mirror movements'.
* Moving shapes of letters of alphabet (ensure the class know where the 'top of the page' is).
* Phonic rhymes (see *Phonic Rhyme Time* by Mary Nash-Wortham – Robinswood Press).
* Timetable stars – as movement, wool patterns.
* Rhythmic passing and receiving bean-bags, or balancing on the head, one on each shoulder, etc., aiming and directing (Classes Two to Three) similar work with tennis balls.
* Finger games (mainly Class One); or games involving independent movement of right and left (Classes Two to Three).
* 'Rod rolling' exercises in pairs and individually.
* String games (see *Pull the Other One* by Michael Taylor – Hawthorn Press).
* Songs and rhymes accelerating slowly to top speed then slowly decelerating (calming) or stopping suddenly at a signal (this can be therapeutic for bed wetters).
* Rhymes or songs where parts are progressively missed out then added again.
* As above but for movement exercises.
* Reverse sequences (essential for timetables, but also possible with verses, etc.)
* Blindfold games (better done, where possible, with eyes closed), seeking sounds, identifying voice or sounding object, use of touch (for example, to identify object, alphabet form or number, etc.).
* Variations of 'Kim's games' (recollecting a collection of items accurately – also those which have been removed from the group).

* Rhythmic clapping and stepping.
* Body geography. Class One: mainly directions for one side then the other; Class Two: mainly directions given for both sides together, including crossing; Class Three: mainly more complicated versions, including giving the instruction then counting 'one, two, three, now!' (Holding on to the instruction develops healthy antipathy.)
* Concentration exercises, especially involving progressive or sequential 'missing out' – deconstruct-reconstruct!

Recall: 'Why' and some alternatives to 'how'

Recall is a fundamental part of the Morning Lesson. That said, it can be one of the most difficult and, as a result, is easily squeezed out. But without active recall the teacher cannot claim to be including the spiritual world, the activity of the night, in the lesson.

Recall time is the moment in the lesson when what is beginning to individualise itself in children through their unconscious communication with the hierarchies, especially the Angels, Archangels and Archai (see, for example, *The Hierarchies as the Source of Action, Speech and Thought*, 28 April 1923, GA224). Paradoxically, then, recall is simultaneously about each child making what they have learned their own *and* developing the class community. Inadequate or absent recall activity leaves the class feeling that what they have been taught skates on the surface of things and locks the emerging 'own-ness' of their learning onto the inarticulate.

Recall time is the class's time, so it needs all the more thought and preparation. It should be homoeopathically brief, potentised and specific, never exhausting, or exhaustive. The artistic rhythmic work that precedes it should serve to ready the class for it. It is not a time for the teacher to repeat what hasn't gone in the day before. And, although there are non-verbal forms of recall, the children need opportunity to speak about what they have learned; inviting individual children to address the class is the fundamental recall activity. Prerequisite to all this is that the teacher had a clear objective for the previous day and seeks to help the class re-enter and explore this quintessence. That may seem relatively easy for skills or questions of knowledge – less so for 'the imponderables', where narrative and image predominate. The subtlest of objectives can be explored through open-ended questions.

Narrative and image are not sufficient unto themselves. They are there to serve the development of the children. The separation suggested above is really a false dichotomy. Stories and images are in the curriculum so that skills can acquire morality and the elements of knowledge can be stirred into vitality. I do not tell the story of Jacob wrestling with the angel simply because it's in the Old Testament and the curriculum indicates Old Testament stories should be for nine-year-olds, or because the class will like the story, but because the image tells of a moment in your development and mine when we attempted to pit our earthly strength and consciousness against the spiritual, as a result of which, like Oedipus, our will is partly lamed. Not that any of what is indicated here will be conveyed directly to the children, but it should serve to help the teacher decide what to recall as well as what skills one might choose to work on with the story.

Free rendering

As recommended by Els Göttgens, this consists of providing the class with a range of materials, coloured and white paper of different sizes, offcuts of fabric, string or wool, alternative drawing materials, glue and scissors, etc. The children are given a precise objective, e.g. 'You have 12 minutes in which to complete a piece of work that shows, in your own way, a pattern that comes about when you divide the circumference of a circle into six equal parts'; or: 'how the Canadian beaver builds its lodge'. The important principle here is that the task is open to the children's initiative but has a precise focus given by the teacher. I feel that it is important that time is provided and encouragement given for individuals to speak about what they have done and what it says about the subject matter. This method can involve work in self-selecting groups (though it may be best to limit their size). Of course, the time allowed may sometimes be ineffecnt, so its helpful to have a strategy in place to ensure the work is completed.

Act it out

Pupils use mime to show part of the story, or to characterise a process described the previous day. The rest of the class put into words what they are being shown.

Acting and seeing

For example, 'Yesterday we heard how Snow White and Rose Red went out together to the river. Which two children can show me how they went?'. Several versions may be shown. Children are asked what they noticed and the 'performers' should explain what made them think that this is the way the two girls skipped, ran, or walked. The essence here might be that they are inseparable, two sides of a coin, for they say, 'We shall always be together, as long as we live', and the mother adds, 'What one has, she must share with the other', which may become a picture and written text for this part of the story. This might invite the exploration of 'all' words (and others) that become one when joined, 'all + ways = always, all + together = altogether, all + ready = already. In other words, a simple introduction to prefixes and suffixes.

Written bursts

The class are given a limited time, say seven minutes, to write down in the most condensed form whatever struck them most from the previous day's presentation. Each pupil then reads and the whole is discussed. (This is a good note-taking practice exercise)

Butting-in

One pupil starts to tell the story to the class (or explain the main points of the previous day). After a short while the speaker must tell a deliberate untruth, at which point the class must say, 'Stop!' and another child continues until they make a deliberate mistake and so on. The teacher must be careful not to confuse 'untruth' with précis (shortening or glossing over detail is not the same as giving false information, a useful distinction when later you deal with note-taking and editing) but must be awake to ensure that an error is not reinforced.

Labels

Each child (or a group) has a 'post-it' type label with a key word from the lesson placed on her or his back. These children do not know what the word is and have to it work out by asking questions that can only be answered with a 'yes', or 'no'. (There are a number of alternative forms for this that can be tailored to the age and character of a class and what needs to be recalled.)

Relevance

The teacher gives a theme, for example, 'James the First'. The pupils then must provide as many words or phrases as they can that pertain *directly* to the theme, so, for this example, 'King of Scotland, James VI, King of Britain, followed Elizabeth I, commissioned a translation of the Bible' would be accepted, but generalised statements, or words like, 'hated Protestants', 'daft', or 'Sir Walter Raleigh' would not, without elaboration or justification. Three or four key words might be given altogether, and the class could use these for written work, but the lists would need some oral 'unpacking' first. This is particularly useful for establishing essential facts or special vocabulary in history or sciences.

Connections

This can be carried out in a similar way, but this time, the class is allowed to add *any* words or phrases that have a connection to the starting point. Indicate who gave the 'connections' and discuss them when each list is 'complete'.

Banyan

One pupil leaves the room. The rest agree on a particular technical word from the subject. The pupil now enters and asks questions. The others answer, but where the agreed word should be used, they substitute the word 'banyan'. The pupil has to guess what the word is.

Vocabulary ping-pong

The class is divided into two teams, 'A' and 'B'. A member of one team and then the other, by turns, have to give a word related to one given by the teacher; these are then written on the blackboard. For example, the class have been studying 'Human physiology and anatomy', the teacher says, 'the eye' and pupil 1A, says, 'retina', 1B says, 'vitreous humour', 2A says, 'iris' and so on. At a certain point, the teacher gives a new topic, for example, 'the ear' and the words now have to relate to this organ. This is a useful summative activity and could be followed by asking the class to sketch one of the sense organs, labelling the parts from a list on the blackboard.

There are many other possibilities, but none of these alternatives should be used too often. 'Basic' oral recall should not be forgotten. The method of recall should be chosen to suit the subject and your teaching aims. Most of these alternatives are less suitable for younger children, but the majority can be adapted to a variety of situations and needs.

18.

Parent and teacher: enthusiasm for education

Whatever may be said about communication, or the lack of it, in the school as a whole, there is one place where it must be paramount: between the adults most immediately and intimately responsible for the child's welfare – parent and teacher.

The parental responsibility is the primary one. Teachers provide education only when parents enable them to do so. The home visit and the class evenings supply the educational side of this relationship. However, this relationship is not always clear; responsibilities become blurred. Divorce or separation is one of the most frequent signs of the way that the destiny of individuals becomes entangled and children are often caught in the snags. Such things may contribute to the tendency for the parents to want, in some ways, to be more like teachers and less like parents to their children. The more complex the relationships in a family, the stronger the tendency, and it is a phenomenon not unknown among Waldorf teachers' families.

The deed of parenting is strongest during the first seven years and is at its most intense in the first three. When interviewing parents before a child joins the class, the teacher should try to arrive at a clear picture of this period of the child's biography; it will often provide helpful insights for

what follows. In their first seven years, children develop on the basis of their genealogy and their environment, most formative of which will be the family home and all that happens there.

The age of authority implies a stepping out from this and the teacher is at first the fosterer (the Spey Women in The King of Ireland's Son) and progressively the interpreter and guide on the way (the role of Raphael in the book of Tobit). Finally the relationship is more like that of a Renaissance Master Artist and the workshop apprentice. Of course the reality of the process is that it cannot be so sharply delineated. For the teacher to work effectively in his or her realm there must be dialogue. The parent and teacher see a child in different lights; and the picture of the whole child can only emerge when these are brought together through understanding of the processes of development at work in a child. But ideas about development should never be superimposed like smoked glass in front of the phenomena the parent or teacher experience. Rather they should grow out of such phenomena as delicate insight raising this or that feature to significance and enabling the adults to act appropriately. The end of year report is of course invaluable in giving a picture of the development over that year.

Suggestions for class evenings

* Involve the children in setting out a display of work. This does not have to be an individual pile of books; it is after all a class evening.
* Give the parents time for browsing through the work. This is a good opportunity for informal conversations, a social moment.
* It can be most helpful to have some activity that the children have had as part of the Morning Lesson that teacher and parents can do together. Give some account of what led to this and why it was chosen, as well as how the class responded. If this is an activity that has a finished object (painting, modelling, etc.), ask the parents whether you could show it to the class the next morning.
* A discussion circle provides opportunity to reflect on this and to share issues to do with the development of the children. It is as valuable for parents to hear how other children in the class are at home as it is for the teacher. A class parent or 'contact' might chair this part of the meeting if this has been prepared beforehand.
* Allow time for informal chat over a cup of tea, with opportunity perhaps to speak about ideas for a class outing or to share photographs of something the class has done recently.
* Set a finishing time and keep to it.
* It is very helpful to have a colleague present for a class evening as an objective eye and ear. If the colleague has taught your class, he or she might make a short presentation as part of the evening, but otherwise can reflect back to the teacher how the evening was received and may well notice anything that was overlooked.
* In any case it is important not to overlook the role of non-Morning Lesson teachers in the education of the children and this needs to be reflected in the agenda of the class evening.
* Home visits will often follow from a class evening. These create the opportunity to talk together at greater length and to enter into the life of the individual child. An aim would be to do this once a year with occasional visits in addition when there are special concerns.
* Finally, be honest: if something did not go well, say so. You are an adult among adults who are all concerned for the children. Resist the temptation to convince of your perfection; you will fail and create disappointment and suspicion. Self-denigration has a similar effect. What's equally important is to set some boundaries. Be open and available but let the parents know, for example, no phone calls at home after 10p.m., or serious conversations five minutes before Morning Lesson is due to start.

Much could be said about the community building side of a Waldorf school. Suffice it to say here that education is the primary task of the school, the adults being drawn together because they share a mutual interest in the appropriate development of the child. Anthroposophy, when it is worn as a badge, is apt to divide people who may have very different perceptions of it, but the child is the real centre.

Enthusiasm for a particular school or group of colleagues is only a beginning. When teachers carry deep conviction that they have a responsibility towards the wider world, they also discover the truth of their dependence, not on their immediate colleagues only, but on the work of Waldorf colleagues everywhere. Flashes and flakes of pedagogical genius are not personal chippings from some block-like tradition, but momentary gifts that the active striving of all – for the potential of all. It is not a matter of *being* a teacher, but of *becoming* one. By enabling the spiritual world to think and act positively for the good, the teacher begins to be not simply one who enjoys community, but becomes a builder of community.

19.

Of meetings and learnings

Rudolf Steiner expected great things of Waldorf teachers, and the school meetings were to be the place from which these great things would receive their inspiration. While our educational work strives to be the highest possible expression of spiritual-cultural goals for our time, our meetings work into, and draw upon, the intentions of the future (see *Towards the Sixth Epoch*). The realisation of this presents an enormous challenge, and the very nature of it indicates that its fulfilment is not to be expected in the immediate, earthly present. But much can be done in the practice of our weekly meetings to bring us closer to a point from which the fulcrum of each individual's spiritual activity can begin to work.

This is not the place to discuss the differentiation of the variety of meetings Waldorf schools tend to have. Anyone who has ever spent any time in one or more of our schools knows what a potential minefield this can be. However, what is relevant to this handbook is the meeting that is variously called the General Staff, Pedagogical or Teachers' Meeting.

Teachers have to work hard individually, both to ensure that they have acquired for themselves what the children need, and to develop and sustain an appropriate relationship with the class.

This would equally be a challenge for the tutor of an individual child. The creation of a school provides a context for a process of education that involves children of different ages and needs and possibilities; something that could not exist in smaller social groups. This whole process involves colleagues.

There is not space here to develop this further, but, the complement between the education of the children and the collegial schooling that is the essential striving of a college of teachers (note I use the word with a small 'c' as a collective noun, not in the form we use commonly to designate a specific group or meeting). Colleges and their activities are not our particular concern here, but rather what can be done with the Teachers' Meeting.

Perhaps the most central task of this meeting is the study of the children, and through this to increase our awareness of child development and to evolve the curriculum accordingly. If we take this seriously, every Teachers' Meeting would include some child or class study.

The outline below is of the possible form that a pedagogical meeting might take.
Standard Agenda example:

* Opening verse
* Colleagues briefly share any pressing concerns
* Overview of agenda
* Child study
* Singing or eurythmy
* Regular points: new children, interviews, health and safety, review of festivals or other events
* Presentation of a Morning Lesson, study for a festival, teacher research (this might also be the space in which a particular concern is taken up, e.g. a bullying policy, preferably after some preparatory papers have been circulated)
* Status reports of work undertaken, correspondence, important information that cannot be given via notice boards or pigeon-holes, delegation of necessary tasks
* A song or simple eurythmy to close and/or
* A verse

One element of such a meeting that sometimes receives short shrift is the child study. We perhaps tend to see this as something performed for a particular child and thus can lament the impossibility of ever studying all the children in a large school. The truth is that no important activity in a school is ever so restricted in it's benefit; what helps the development of all the children, of the school as a whole and of the collegial strength of the institution is that the child study, provided it is carried with the care and attention due to it, is also a schooling of perception. Before starting it would be good to speak to the child's parents indicating the supportive nature of such a study. It might even be possible for the parents to be present at the first stage of such a study and, possibly, an older child might also be asked to attend some part of such a study. It should be a supportive gesture and indicate the high quality of care we give to the children we teach.

I would suggest that child studies take place over two weeks. At Alder Bridge and elsewhere I have experienced a three-stage process, which can be good if done thoroughly, but, on the whole, a three-week child study always risks becoming drawn out, and thus the effect dissipates and attention flags. The extra week also limits – to a greater degree than might be thought, especially when festivals and special events are borne in mind – the number of children who can be studied in this way. For this reason the process below has three stages that can be conducted over two or three weeks.

Guidelines for child study

Stage one

1. Soul Calendar verse corresponding to week of child's birthday is read at the beginning. Possibly a candle may be lit.

2. Describe the child objectively (it can be helpful to show a photo of the child for those in the circle who do not teach the class) including:

    i. Height, weight, build, proportions;
    ii. How does the child sit, stand, walk, and run? (Colleagues may attempt to imitate these, describing their observations and what qualities they perceive);
    iii. Facial expression and gaze;
    iv. Other features (eyes, nose, ears, and hands…);
    v. Laterality.

3. Speech qualities: volume, pitch, modulation and flow and any disturbances such as stammering or sounds incorrectly pronounced.

4. Thinking qualities: memory, imagination, practical intelligence, and ability to learn.

5. Feeling qualities: enthusiasm or apathy, friendships and other significant relationships, emotional response, fears.

6. Will qualities: ability to see something through once started, strong likes or dislikes towards foods, initiative, assertiveness.

7. Brief background/biography: show some characteristic school work (both good and bad).

N.B. If there is plenty of time, in special circumstances some of the above might be dramatised or drawing might be used to indicate certain qualities.

Stage two

1. Soul Calendar.

2. Briefly review then characterise.

3. Constitution, temperament, character type (adolescents).

4. If the child were a landscape, a plant, an animal, which one would they be and why?

5. From Class Six upwards, imagine the child in a particular cultural epoch or historical setting – again, which, what and why? (All colleagues help to build these pictures trying to avoid any unconscious sympathy or antipathy by being aware of this danger for one another.)

6. Finally if the child has a birthday verse this should be read by the teacher with some indication of the intentions within it.

Stage three

*   What is this child asking of me as a teacher and of us all as colleagues in the school?
*   Shorter one-off studies of a whole class or group of children may also be held.

Appendices

Some of these worksheets
and checklists are available to download from

www.florisbooks.co.uk/books/Steiner-Waldorf-Handbook

Appendix A:
Movement skills

Development of motor proficiency and approximate ages

Normally at:

4 months   The Moro Reflex (the babies' primitive 'flight or fight' reaction) is replaced by an adult-style 'startle reflex'.

6 months   The child holds head erect easily; rotational movement possible. Supports body on outstretched arms. Can transfer object from one hand to the other. Asymmetric Tonic Neck Reflex[16] is inhibited.

7 months   Momentarily holds trunk in erect sitting position. Assumes crawl position.

9 months   Spinal Gallant Reflex inhibited (from 3 months). Is able to hold trunk erect for long periods in sitting position. Assumes creeping position on hands and knees.

11 months   Walks about using supports, chairs etc. Symmetric Tonic Neck Reflex is normally inhibited by this age.

13 months   Attains proficiency in releasing and dropping objects.

18 months   Stands unsupported with weight on both feet. If reaching for objects, places opposite hand on furniture for balance. Tonic Neck Reflex is overcome.

21 months   Begins to run, and can climb stairs alone.

2 years   Can imitate clapping – a bilateral movement. Uses alternation of steps over an obstacle while walking. Protective arm extension is now automatic (e.g. when falling).

3 years   Stands on one foot momentarily. Can jump down from a step. With two feet together, jumps out with one foot leading, able to ride tricycle. By 3.5 years Tonic Labyrinthine Reflex should be inhibited.

4 years   Takes pleasure in swinging, spinning, whirling. Can duck-walk, squat and grasp with thumb and middle finger, and thumb and index finger. Horizontal mid-line is crossed.

5 years Horizontal mid-line is established so arm swing co-ordinates with jump (for example). Marches to music, can begin tying bow knot, catch bean bag in a bucket, bounce a ball, log roll, tap to match beat, and pick up small objects with finger-thumb opposition.

6–7 years Consistent two-footed jump becomes automatic. Can balance on one foot with eyes closed. Movement of head, trunk, arms, hands and feet differentiated. Can oppose all fingers to the thumb precisely with eyes open or shut. Left and right established for self. Eye-hand co-ordination is refined so eye leads the hand. Increased movement of hand at wrist and foot at ankle. Can accomplish two motor tasks simultaneously. Language localisation in the hemispheres is taking place.

8 years Arms have automatic reciprocal movement as in pulling oneself upright: no longer bilateral arm pull. Increased upper torso strength. Can use reciprocal movement with one part of the body as upper torso and bilateral with lower body as in sloth hang on bar or beam, or butterfly stroke in swimming (one of the reasons this is the fastest learning age for swimming strokes). Can accomplish difficult spatial relationships such as the hop, skip

and jump sequence. Serial memory is good, so students can complete a sequence of run, vault, straddle roll, forward roll from one command. Eye-hand co-ordination is precise.

N.B. The above is not intended as a 'checklist', but provides some insight into the normal pattern of motor development. This is included in order to provide a context for the movement skills and 'warning signs' indicated elsewhere. For more information see *Reflexes, Learning and Behavior* by Sally Goddard (Fern Ridge Press).

Handedness and speech

There is a lemniscatory, or crossing, action involved in the perception and co-ordination of movement. The left-hand side of the brain is involved with actions on the right-hand side of the body and vice versa. The activity of speech is usually associated with the left hemisphere of the brain in right-handed people; this may be reversed for most left-handers.

Appendix B:
Indicators of possible
special learning needs

Tick the items that apply. Most of the items shown below would apply at *any* age. Where possible, it would be helpful to ask the parents to fill out a copy of the checklist independently in order to compare the results. This checklist is not quantitative, but clearly the more points ticked, the more certain one can be of the potential difficulty. It is important to try to establish the objective signs on which your judgment is based. A specialist teacher, or a qualified educational psychologist should be consulted if, having completed the checklist, you feel there are evident difficulties that need more specific identification.

Academic indicators

* Poor spelling
* Poor reading aloud
* Poor reading comprehension
* Confusion or reversal of letters and/or numbers
* Poor sentence structure (speaking and/or writing)
* Weak expressive vocabulary
* Hesitant speech
* Flat or monotonous speech
* Inability to sing in tune
* Unable to remember sequences (days of week, months of the year, etc.)
* Discrepancies between ability in range of basic skills

Motor skills

* Poor body use (posture and general mobile stance)
* Weak body geography
* Poor spatial orientation
* Fidgets a great deal
* Continuing confusion of right and left
* Messy handwriting
* Uncertain or mixed dominance
* Clumsy, unco-ordinated movements
* Difficulties in organising self and personal possessions, etc.
* Poor sense of rhythm
* Poor skills in games and other physical activities
* Incorrect pencil grip

Receptive listening

* Short attention span
* Easily distracted
* Inability to follow a sequence of instructions (e.g. able to 'remember only one or two items from a sequence of three or four')

* Misinterpretation of questions
* Need for frequent repetition
* Confusion of similar-sounding words
* Oversensitive to sounds

Social skills

* Low tolerance of frustration
* Poor self-esteem
* Excessive shyness or inability to accommodate the needs of others
* Difficulty in making friends
* Irritability
* Immaturity
* Indicates feeling overburdened with everyday tasks
* Low motivation
* Negative attitude towards schoolwork

Qualities of will

* Difficulties getting up in the morning
* Difficulties in getting to sleep, or settling down at night
* Frequently expresses tiredness
* Hyperactivity
* Frequent procrastination

Background information

Great care needs to be taken with this. The information would usually be given in the course of the initial interview, or during a home visit, and may help to provide insights into some of the circumstances of the way the difficulty manifests.

* Stressful pregnancy
* Difficult birth
* Early separation from mother
* Adoption

* Delay in developing language
* Recurring ear infections
* Any family history of learning difficulties

Classes One and Two: detailed assessment

Warning signs

Many a class teacher, having used a checklist for Class One readiness, might find it helpful to refer back to it during the course of the first two terms to see which factors, omitted during the original assessment, develop during that time. A static picture would be the first thing to alert one's concern.

The following is a checklist for the teacher to use during the first and second years to help detect whether a child's development is lagging behind. Where possible a colleague trained in spatial dynamics should be consulted. An assistant is recommended – ideally the learning support teacher – to help with the more detailed observations.

The child's parents should also be aware of this. In most cases, where there are a number of such symptoms, a learning support teacher and/or school doctor should be consulted too. This provides a detailed assessment, but much of it would need to be administered by a suitably qualified teacher and in a one-to-one situation.

The following checklist is intended for use by class teachers in the context of their normal classroom work. The teacher needs to be aware of which activities will enable certain observations to be made and in the case of large classes the children may be grouped or observed row by row. Look for patterns or habitual and persistent problems. Every child may show some indication of learning difficulties at some time and isolated instances are not significant; repeated occurrences should be noted, and acted upon.

A child *may* have a specific learning difficulty if he or she shows a number of the following symptoms as a repeated pattern of behaviour.

Class One

* Excessive or deficient response to sounds
* Markedly poor discrimination between words or speech sounds
* Timidity (may fear heights, slides, stairs, swings) or show lack of caution in dangerous situations
* Lethargy, listlessness, inactivity
* Clumsiness – often bumps into things
* Retention of baby words (baby quality to speech)
* Tendency to accidental spoonerisms
* Excessive reliance on routine; upset by change
* Lack of rhythm in speech, walk, singing
* Inability to recognise rhyme
* Marked continuation of generalised grammatical rules ('we keeped this at home', 'they selled it to me', etc.)
* Too firm a grasp of a pencil, or held with a strange grip (have the children been taught how to do this properly?)

Class Two

* Continues to confuse up and down, under and over, back and front
* Continues to confuse left and right (in relation to themselves and/or surrounding space)
* Continues to have difficulty with hopping, skipping, balancing, jumping

* Is erratic (good days and bad days with no evident cause)
* Poor spacing of work
* Poor handwriting
* Poor body geography
* Does not 'get' relevant jokes or riddles
* Confuses recall of stories/Morning Lesson material
* Chooses younger or much older children for play companions
* Has memory difficulties, especially with sequences (auditory or visual)
* With eyes closed, fails to point correctly to prominent objects in room (i.e. blackboard)
* Ongoing difficulty with right/left symmetrical drawing, indicating little or no sense for the *completion* of form
* Tinny and poorly inflected speech tone
* No indication of an awareness of the 'audience' when speaking to others

Specific motor control (Class Two)
Ball Games:

* How does the child throw a ball?
* How does the child catch a ball?
* Is he/she fearful of the ball?
* Does he/she see it coming?
* Can he/she throw or catch better?
* Does this relate to social situations?

'Returning' beanbags, e.g., the children may throw the bags as the teacher holds a basket:

* Describe how the child does this. (Note which hand is used, the angle of head in relation to the hand, signs of tension in throwing, etc.)
* Is there a holding back in the throw? (What is the quality of intention here?)

* How is balance affected by the throw?
* What does the no-throwing hand do?

How does the child balance on a log or balance beam?

* Can she/he walk backwards as well as forwards?
* Can she/he balance on one leg?
* Which leg is chosen? (Is it different to the dominant hand? Is this a regular choice?)

Observe the children skipping:

* Do the knees bend? Is there a rigidity in the movement?
* Is balance retained in the movement, or is there a feeling of being continually falling forward?
* Do the feet work together? (Is there a lop-sidedness?)
* Are arms and legs synchronised?

Writing with the feet:

* Observe what the feet are like (notice any stiffness, immobile toes).
* Do the child's hands or mouth move while attempting to do this?
* Which foot is used? Is it different to the dominant hand?

'Shaking' hands:

* Ask the child to squeeze your hand. Watch the other hand. Infantile reflex is for the other hand to open; mature laterality is indicated by the other hand remaining free.
* Which hand is offered? Is there any confusion as to which to use?

Play a body geography game:

* Observe what happens when instruction requires crossing (e.g. 'touch left knee with right hand', touch ears, eyes, shoulders, elbows, etc.)

Hand-eye co-ordination when form drawing:

* Do the eyes follow the hand as it traces a shape in the air?
* Is there excessive movement of the head?
* Do the eyes track smoothly through the midline?

Sequencing:

* How does the child respond to instructions?
* Is there any tendency to 'hear' only the last thing said if the instructions have two or three elements?
* Can the child place objects in order (e.g. tidying books according to size or colour, etc.)?

Observations based on the above may indicate the need to carry out a formal assessment, preferably with the school doctor. Ask the child to draw a person and keep this with the child's file. The way in which this is done can often provide the teacher with helpful diagnostic information. The Goodenough-Harris scale on page 100 can be used to provide a more detailed analysis. No comment should be made about this to the child. Drawing of archetypal images such as house, tree and person may also provide helpful indicators. (For a detailed alternative, see Appendix C, 'The seven-element picture' on page 103.) Alerted to difficulties in the areas indicated here, the teacher has a duty to draw concerns to the attention of parents. Where there are problems in a number of areas, or where these are profound, a professional *assessment* should always be sought. The fact that a child is not disruptive or apparently suffering should not persuade a class teacher to proceed with such a child without suitable learning support.

Appendix C:
An interpretive device

The Goodenough-Harris test

Directions

'I want you to make a picture of a person. Make the very best picture that you can. Take your time and work very carefully. Try very hard and see what a good picture you can make.'

Time

No time limit. Usually 10 minutes will suffice with young children. This test is to be used primarily as a screening device. The drawings of bright children more than 10 years old, or those who have had drawing lessons, will result in an invalid evaluation of the child's intellectual potential.

Scoring

Class A

Preliminary stage in which the drawing cannot be recognised as a human figure:

* Aimless uncontrolled scribbling – score 0.
* Lines somewhat controlled – approaches crude geometrical form – score 1.

Class B

All drawings can be recognised as attempts to represent the human figure. Each bulleted item is scored plus or minus. One point is given for each plus and no half-credits are given:

Gross detail
* Head present
* Legs present
* Arms present
* Trunk present
* Length of trunk greater than breadth
* Shoulders are indicated (abrupt broadening of trunk below neck)

Attachments
* Both arms and legs attached to trunk
* Arms and legs attached to trunk at correct points
* Neck present
* Outline of neck continuous with that of head, trunk, or both

Head detail
* Eyes present (one or two)
* Nose present

* Mouth present
* Nose and mouth in two dimensions, two lips shown
* Nostrils shown
* Hair shown
* Hair on more than circumference of head and non-transparent – better than a scribble

Clothing

* Clothing present (any clear representation of clothing)
* Two articles of clothing non-transparent (excluding hat, trousers)
* Entire drawing free from transparencies – sleeves and trousers must be shown
* Four articles of clothing definitely indicated (should include four – hat, shoes, coat, shirt, necktie, belt, trousers)
* Costume complete with incongruities (business suit, soldier's costume – hat, sleeves trousers and shoes must be shown)

Hand detail

* Fingers present (any indication)
* Correct number of fingers shown
* Fingers in two dimensions – length greater than breadth, angle subtended not greater than 180 degrees
* Opposition of thumb clearly defined
* Hand shown distinct from fingers and arm

Joints

* Arm joint shown – elbow, shoulder, or both
* leg joint shown – knee, hip, or both

Proportion

* Head not more than half or less than one tenth of trunk
* Arms equal to trunk but not reaching knee

* Legs not less than trunk not more than twice trunk size
* Feet in two dimensions – not more than one third or less than one tenth of leg
* Both arms and legs in two dimensions

Motor co-ordination

* Lines firm without marked tendency to cross, gap, or overlap
* All lines firm with correct joining
* Outline of head without obvious irregularities. Develop beyond first crude circle. Conscious control apparent
* Trunk outline. Score same as number three
* Arms and legs without irregularities. Two dimensions and no tendency to narrow at point of junction with trunk
* Features symmetrical (more likely to credit in profile drawings)

Fine head detail

* Ears present (two in full face, one in profile)
* Ears present in correct position and proportion
* Eye detail – brow or lashes shown
* Eye detail – pupil shown
* Eye detail – proportion. Length greater than width
* Eye detail – glance – only plus in profile
* Chin and forehead shown

Profile

* Projection of chin shown – usually plus in profile
* Heel clearly shown
* Body profile – head, trunk, and feet without error
* Figure shown in true profile without error or transparency

The following table shows the estimated age of cognitive maturity (CM):

SCORE	CM	SCORE	CM	SCORE	CM	SCORE	CM
1	3–3	14	6–6	27	9–9	40	13–0
2	3–6	15	6–9	28	10–0	41	13–3
3	3–9	16	7–0	29	10–3	42	13–6
4	4–0	17	7–3	30	10–6	43	13–9
5	4–3	18	7–6	31	10–9	44	14–0
6	4–6	19	7–9	32	11–0	45	14–3
7	4–9	20	8–0	33	11–3	46	14–6
8	5–	21	8–3	34	11–6	47	14–9
9	5–3	22	8–6	35	11–9	48	15–0
10	5–6	23	8–9	36	12–0	49	15–3
11	5–9	24	9–0	37	12–3	50	15–6
12	6–0	25	9–3	38	12–6	51	15–9
13	6–3	26	9–6	39	12–9		

In finding the IQ of children with learning disabilities who are more than 13 years old, the chronological age should be treated as 13 only, and the IQ recorded as 'or below'.

It is not wise to attempt to use this test with bright children of more than 12 years of age.

The 'seven-element picture' – an interpretive device

This is a markedly different procedure to that for the Goodenough-Harris test. The interpretation of children's artistic work for therapeutic purposes requires specific training. However, to look at a drawing with an artistic eye, in order to discern something of the developmental artist in the child, is possible for any teacher seeking to practise an art of education.

Looking at children's artwork in this way is a sensitive matter, not one of scientific precision. The teacher searches for characteristic qualities much in the way a good communicator responds to the tone of a conversation. Teachers, especially at interview, frequently use the 'house' picture. The outline below suggests a more differentiated approach that may be helpful to supplement or provide other observations for the teacher to work with. More important than the discrete elements of the picture indicated here is the balance of the whole thing, the overall impression. The elements themselves can give useful pointers to what is working within the child with regard to the qualities indicated. But on no account should these indications be treated in the manner of pseudo-Freudian determinators of inner state, any more than when a child who goes through a period of using large quantities of paint should have to bear the label of being identified authoritatively as a 'dark soul'.

The seven elements the children may be asked to use when composing a picture are:

* Sun   * Path   * Snake   * Bird
* Hill   * Water   * Tree

Children may add other features, but these seven must appear. The interpretive indications are as follows:

* **Sun** – may be taken as a picture of the connection with the spiritual. Consider whether the sun is drawn large or small, whether clouds cover it, and the quality of the colour and luminosity.

* **Hill** – may give an indication of the child's sense of (mainly unconscious) goals. Are they barren and uninviting, or do they draw the observer towards them? Are they distinct or partly veiled?

* **Path** – may indicate a sense of the quality of the route towards the 'goal'.

* **Water** – may give a picture of unconscious qualities. Consider how much of the picture this takes up and the quality of its appearance.

* **Snake** – may indicate basal or 'animal' energy, suggesting the way in which the unconscious (water) qualities are embodied.

* **Tree** – may indicate the self's picture of itself (think of the world tree of Norse mythology). Consider its uprightness or otherwise, the way it relates to the rest of the picture, whether covered in leaves or is wintry, etc.

* **Bird** – may indicate something of the sense of the quality of freedom.

The 'eighth element'

Many children are likely to spontaneously add a human figure, or a house, or both. In either case, or even when both appear, these representations may signify the self in its relation to the different elements indicated above, and its own sense of worth, security and harmony or any lack of these qualities.

N.B. This is interpretative, not diagnostic.

Appendix D:
A possible foundation script

The handwriting shown here has been slightly adapted from one designed specifically for children with dyslexia. It has some useful features that make it, I believe, applicable for whole classes.

The principle here is that all words can be completed without the need to lift the writing implement from the page ('i's, 't's, 'j's and 'x's have dots or strokes added once the word has been written. The 'x' is the most controversial here; see below). Provided the essential features are retained, it is possible to adapt this alphabet further (e.g. upper loops might be added), but the teacher should be aware of the reasons for this and not simply follow the line of least resistance (or her, or his own habits).

a tree stood in the wild wood

* All lower loops (rhythmicity into the 'will zone') are *clockwise* (not usually the case for 'f')
* The open 'b' helps to reinforce a distinction between 'b' and 'd'.
* Every word can be completed without lifting the pen or pencil (helping to reinforce kinaesthetic memory – the 'movement memory' of the flow and shape of the word).
* Slant is upright to forward.
* Though this can be changed, in the version given here, the upper 'thinking' zone involves no loop but a concentrating repetition of the vertical.

N.B. The 'x' form has some special considerations, like 's' it depends on the letter that stands before it.

abcdefghijklmnopqrstuvwxyz

Essential features

All letters have connectors; a lead-in stroke is part of the letter, even when it stands on it own. For example:

cross cross

except { *lift pen only once*
except { *word is complete – then*
         add cross

or (completed) ox
are (completed) axe

105

Appendix E:
Number orientation

While the reversal of letterforms is reasonably common at the beginning of Class One (the persistence of the tendency should always indicate the need to examine whether there are other indicators of special needs), the reversal of numbers is sometimes overlooked. There are various ways to help children arrive at a correct orientation of letters, cursive writing being one of them. Since there are no cursive numbers, teaching their correct orientation is all the more important. The following suggestion may be found helpful:

These numbers look back towards heaven:

Heaven				Earth
Window >	↖1	↖2	↖3	< Door
Past				Future

These numbers look towards the future:

Heaven				Earth
Window >	4↗	5↗	6↗	< Door
Past				Future

Seven and nine look back towards the three previous numbers, with eight holding the balance.

Heaven				Earth
Window >	7	8	9	< Door
Past				Future

Why not vary these according to the orientation of your classroom and create your own pictures.

N.B. This works well for the number forms shown here. The closed form of figure 4 is less suited to this approach.

Appendix F:
Self-evaluation form

This form can be used in a number of ways. Ideally it would feature as a part of a process of collegial intervision, each of a pair, or triad, of teachers making a self-evaluation privately, and then sharing it with their partner(s). Comparing this with the impressions of a visiting colleague would be the best way to complete the process. Alternatively, it can be used simply as an aid to a teacher's personal appraisal of their classroom work. While some teachers may wish to complete the form in one sitting, it is designed in such a way that each main section may be used on three, preferably consecutive, days.

During the course of a week, take time to consider the following questions in order to review your teaching. Decide well ahead of the date which week you intend to conduct this self-evaluation (there is little point in simply choosing a good week as the basis for your review). Use the form to assess your strengths and weaknesses. While the former should be celebrated, it is the latter that are most interesting. These are opportunities for development, if we choose to take them. In order to do this, the 'further action' section of the questionnaire needs to be as practical possible. Each school should have a 'staff development budget' to facilitate a professional approach to these matters. The SWSF advisory service can also be consulted and, in some cases, staff study days or ongoing development work can also be honed to answer the common areas of need for in-service education.

Part I: Picturing the whole situation

1. Form as vivid a picture as you can of today's Morning Lesson from the moment you arrived in the classroom. Put yourself in the position of an invisible visitor, or fly-on-the-wall. Briefly describe: the appearance of the room, the work on display, seasonal table, any work on the blackboard, arrangement of desks, etc.:

2. Move on to picturing yourself in the room, your actions and any preparation. Picture also how the children arrive. How do you greet them and how do they respond? Carry these recollections to the point where you call the register. Note down your observations:

3. Picture the course of the Morning Lesson to its end. Recollect your own actions and interaction with individual children and the class as a whole. Picture your own movements in class, how you stand at the front, how you use the blackboard, etc. Notice any tensions, or moments when your attention was divided. Notice, too, moments when you and the class seemed to be moving as one. Note your observations:

4. Finally, consider what the class did during the lesson. What was the balance between your direction and organisation and that of the children? Are the class self-sufficient in dealing with everyday arrangements; giving out books, checking spelling in the dictionary, etc. Who worked hardest during the various parts of the lesson?

5. Summarise any points from the above you consider significant. What do you feel is going well? What things would you like to change?

6. Further action:

Part II: The shape and rhythm of the Morning Lesson

1. What were my aims and objectives for this lesson?

2. How were these realised?

3. How did I prepare this lesson? What was unexpected? What needed greater preparation?

4. Make a representation of the path of the lesson. What observations would you make with regard to its 'flow' and the transition moments? What moods were present during the lesson? Did the children find something to laugh about? Were there quiet and active moments? What did you observe about the class during the moment just before you closed the lesson? Did you address any particular temperaments through the way in which you presented something or asked questions?

5. What problem area(s) did I encounter?

6. How did I deal with these?

7. What new theme, skill, content, etc., did I present today?

8. How did the class respond?

9. What aspects of movement did I employ today?

10. How did the class respond?

11. In what way did music or speech feature in the lesson?

12. In what way did the class engage with these?

13. In what way did drawing, colour or modelling feature in the lesson?

14. In what way did the class engage with this?

15. What was my recall activity?

16. How did the class respond?

17. In what ways were the children active during the lesson?

18. Could the class be helped to be more self-responsible for any aspect of classroom management?

19. Did some aspect of the lesson challenge every child? Which children (if any) did I not notice today?

20. Which children (if any) seem to have absorbed more attention than others?

21. Why?

22. How do you record what the children have learned?

23. How would you characterise communication with, and from, the class's parents?

24. How would you characterise communication with colleagues?

25. Summarise anything from the above that you feel to be significant. What do you feel is going well? What would you wish to change?

26. Further action:

Teaching Skills Summary

Key: Numbers in the key boxes below are repeated in the alphabetical lists and may be circled or otherwise highlighted for clarity and speed of assessment.

1	2	3	4	5
I lack basic skills or training in this area	I am not very confident about this; I need support	I have sufficient skills and confident to identify what I need to do	I am reasonably confident in my skills and experience	I could offer help to others with this area

A. Lesson material appropriate for the class:

1	2	3	4	5

B. Creating a good working atmosphere in the class:

1	2	3	4	5

C. Setting clear and obtainable objectives for the class:

1	2	3	4	5

D. Use of blackboard:

1	2	3	4	5

E. Use of voice:

1	2	3	4	5

G. Use of movement:

1	2	3	4	5

H. Storytelling/working with narrative:

1	2	3	4	5

I. Pacing of the lesson:

1	2	3	4	5

J. Coaching individual children/ meeting specific needs:

1	2	3	4	5

K. Communication with parents:

1	2	3	4	5

Key to Summary	Development approach – individual and school supported plan	Review – note and date
1		
2		
3		
4		
5		
6		
7		
8		
9		
10		
11		
12		

This part of the evaluation may be used as the 'public' part of the exercise. While the above should remain in the hands of the teacher concerned (even when used in a peer review), this single sheet could form the basis of any individual staff development plan.

A larger version is available to download at www.florisbooks.co.uk/books/Steiner-Waldorf-Handbook

Appendix G:
Planners and record sheets

Teachers will have their own methods of recording their preparations. Occasionally these consist of a detailed list of items for the Morning Lesson, but sometimes there is little else. The forms that follow are not intended to replace personal notes. Instead they provide an overview of the day ahead with points for reminders in an accessible form. While the items in this section are 'planners', it should be remembered that such plans, especially if modified when something different happens, constitute a valuable daily record of the main activities of each day in a form that takes very little time to maintain.

The Year Planner provides a similar overview of the whole Morning Lesson programme and it is intended that this would be completed during the summer preparation period before the school year begins. Failure to carry out such an overview (which may have to be amended) tends to result in certain areas of the curriculum being omitted. Ideally, there should always be time set aside during pre-term meetings for colleagues to share their planning with one another.

These resources are also available at www.florisbooks.co.uk/books/Steiner-Waldorf-Handbook

Daily lesson overview

Date:
Objectives/priorities:

	Lessons/Activities	Equipment/room needed
A.M. Class		
P.M. Class		
Break times/duties	**After school/meetings**	**Personal reminders**

Daily lesson planner

Date: Class: Lesson:

* Lesson Objectives:

    * What is to be *recalled*?
    * What is to be *practised*?
    * What *new learning* do you intend?

* Main content (indicate time to be spent on each element):

* What will the class do?

* Pupils to observe (areas to note):

After the lesson:

* What happened? (Observations only):

* Important points for the next lessons:

* Pupil observations:

* Evaluation:

Year planner

Date: Class: For year: Overall aims and objectives for the year:

Date	Theme	Summary	Comments, festivals, etc	Date	Theme	Summary	Comments, festivals, etc	Date	Theme	Summary	Comments, festivals, etc

Lesson planning sheet

Theme or subject: Dates:

Monday	Tuesday	Wednesday	Thursday	Friday

Comments:

Summarise overall aims (e.g., to develop awareness of rhythm of English language):

Specific goals/objectives (e.g., teach use of full stop, capital letters):

Intended approach (e.g., to lead from stepping of sentences composed with the class – clap stops, jump capitals, etc. – to written form):

N.B. This planner is intended to give an overview of the week. The learning goals in the 'Daily lesson planner' (page 115) are perhaps the most important part of this.

Appendix H:
Record keeping for individual children

Subject lesson planning and record sheet

School year:

Teacher:

Period:

Date:

Class:

(for example, first half-term, September to October)

Objectives for this period

	Comments/outcomes
Eurythmy	
Music/singing	
Painting	
Form drawing	
Modelling	
Handwork/craft	
French	
German	
Numeracy	
Literacy	

Summary for Morning Lesson and other subjects

(to be used in combination with the preceding form)

School year:
Teacher:

Child:
Class:

	Sep	Oct	Nov	Dec	Jan	Feb	Mar	Apr	May	Jun	Jul
Morning Lesson											
Understanding											
Pace of work											
Handwriting											
Spelling											
Involvement											
Presentation											
Homework											
Self-reliance											
Other /general comments											
Painting											
Colour											
Form											
Involvement											
Independence											

	Sep	Oct	Nov	Dec	Jan	Feb	Mar	Apr	May	Jun	Jul
Music											
Singing											
Instruments											
Technique											
Involvement											
Independence											
Homework/practice											
Handwork											
Technique											
Planning											
Involvement											
Independence											
Foreign language											
Vocabulary											
Understanding											
Homework											
Independence											
Involvement											
Pronunciation											
Grammar											
Spelling											
Bookwork											

	Sep	Oct	Nov	Dec	Jan	Feb	Mar	Apr	May	Jun	Jul
Foreign language											
Vocabulary											
Understanding											
Homework											
Independence											
Involvement											
Pronunciation											
Grammar											
Spelling											
Bookwork											
Eurythmy											
Technique											
Movement											
Involvement											
Independence											
Other / general comments											

Other practice lesson												
Spelling												
Punctuation												
Style												
Vocabulary												
Handwriting												
Reckoning												
Accuracy												
Drawing												
Problem-solving												
Social skills												
Attitude												

Comments and general observations:

_____

_____

N.B. This form can easily be adapted to the needs of particular teachers. It is only an indication, and it would be best for each school to create its own version. It is worthwhile noting, however, that a consolidated form, such as the one shown here, ought to be held in the child's official file (held as part of the school's records, not simply in individual teacher folders). The putting together of the full summary could easily be part of the annual report-writing process and should make this much easier.

The blank recordsheet that appears on the opposite page can be adapted to what teachers are frequently asked for during HMI visits. Used well, such a form can be an important aid for teaching, irrespective of outer demands. The lists of objectives and skills indicated in Section Two of this handbook could be used to provide column titles, with the children's names in the first row. The key is then used to summarise how each child has managed to grasp the specified skill or knowledge (other types of notation can be used, but, personally, I have found the five point scheme indicted here the most practical).

Setting out the main objectives and skills in this way serves two purposes: to facilitate the monitoring of pupil progress in order to provide more focused help or greater challenge when needed; and to assist in the thinking through of what skills and abilities the children need to acquire in order to cope with the demands of the subject, both immediately and in the longer term. These formative objectives (towards understanding where the children are and to encourage clarity in preparation) are surely worthwhile in their own right, irrespective of any other requirements.

There are several examples to follow, which slow specific subject and class objectives.

Similar skills lists can be made for singing, painting, etc., based on checklists in Section One.

From Classes Five to Six onwards, Morning Lesson assessments can be introduced that are increasingly more formal in style (providing an opportunity to prepare basic exam technique) and pupils can be asked for a self-assessment and lesson evaluation. This summative appraisal, however, needs to stand within regular informal, semi-formal and structured assessment.

Blank forms can be downloaded from www.florisbooks.co.uk/books/Steiner-Waldorf-Handbook

Key:

1. Very secure. Can apply knowledge to relevant situations, able to help others, needs new challenges
2. Generally secure. More practice may be needed, especially in challenging areas
3. Understands but needs practice to consolidate skills etc.
4. Tends to be uncertain or confused, needs help to understand process, regular practice required
5. Cause for concern, likely to need individual help (check prior skills)

Record sheet: Key skills

Teacher:

Class:

Name and date												

Example: Class Two Mathematics

Name	Count to 100 in sequence	Accurate counting objects	Knows number bonds to 20	Can apply number to 10s	Can count in 2s to 100	Can count in 5s to 100	Correct notation for tens, units	Correct notation HTU and the HTU
Arion								
Flora								
Hygiea								
Linus								

Name	'x' times table in sequence	'x' times table reverse	'x' times table random	Repeat previous for each	Looks for pattern	Translates numbers into	Vice versa	Correct use of pounds and pence	Makes sensible predictions
Arion									
Flora									
Hygiea									
Linus									

General observations and responses

Teacher: Class:

Name and date	Observation	Action to be taken (further exercises or other support)

Record sheet: Speaking and listening (mainly for Classes One to Three)[17]

Teacher:

Class:

Key: score from 1–5, with 1 indicating high level of skill, ability, positivity, and 5 indicating cause for concern.
Use reverse for observations and interventions.

Name and date	Able to attend to stories	Responds to narrative and imagery	Follows clear instructions correctly	Enters the mood of a narrative	Shares news, etc. with class	Speaks using sentences/ complete utterances	Listens readily to others in class	Engages in conversation (give and take)	Takes part in recitation	Solo recitation

Record sheet: Handwriting

Teacher:

Class:

Name and date	Formation	Rhythm	Speed	Layout	Posture	Attitude	Observations

Handwriting: some points to consider

Formation

Reversals (which letters?), slant (upright, to right or left, random, any extreme), shaping of individual letters, lead-in strokes, start and end point, connections, size (too big, too small, uneven), mixing print and cursive, loops or lack of loops.

Rhythm

Flow or lack of flow, evidence of pressure or lack of pressure (indicated by heaviness of strokes), spacing of letters and words, quality of movement over the page (any tendency to pause).

Speed

Slow, measured, quick, rushed.

Layout

Appearance of whole page, margins (right, left, above, below), tendency to 'taper', use of colour, decoration, awareness of line breaks, paragraphs etc.

Attitude

Antipathy or enthusiasm, rejection of own work, unmotivated, feeling for aesthetics of handwriting (or lack of this).

This form is convenient for your summary. The best way to gather the observations is to have a notebook on your desk with a page for each main area, e.g. handwriting, reading, spelling, speech, form drawing, number, general observations, discussions with parents.

Record sheet: Reading (early stages)

Teacher:

Class:

Name and date	Reading known text	Reading of individual words from known text (out of context)	Sounds letters correctly for unknown words	Makes informed guesses from context	Builds words using phonics	Regularly tries unknown words	Observations

Record sheet: Silent reading
(middle of Class Three onwards)

Teacher: Class:

Name and date	Comprehension	Speed	Attention	Memory	Observations

Silent reading: some points to consider

Comprehension

Level of complexity of text, interest, ability to predict what may happen next, inability to keep track of plot (other than what has just been read).

Attention

For how long can reading be sustained (irrespective of reading ability), superficiality or depth, whether time is needed to 'get into the process', tendency to wander away from reading (literally or inwardly), whether better able to read aloud than silently.

Memory

Whether able to recall accurately the following day, continuous need to refer back to previous pages (names, plot situations, etc.), whether able to retain the whole when explaining a part, long-term and short-term recollection.

Observations/attitude

Enjoyment or lack of enjoyment, selection of reading matter, unable to let go or reluctant to start.

Record sheet: 'Free' writing or own compositions (Class Three onwards[18])

Teacher: Class:

Name	Vocabulary	Punctuation and spelling	Sentence structure	Content	Observations

Record sheet: Speech

Teacher: Class:

Name and date	Articulation	Breath and rhythm (including use of pauses, quality of phrasing)	Expression (including intonation, variety of pace, etc)	Projection	Attitude	Observations

Appendix I:
When nothing seems to be working

The lists of points in Section Two will give a daily formative evaluation during the course of a Morning Lesson and the self-evaluation form may also be helpful. Wrestling meditatively with a few paragraphs from *Allgemeine Menschenkunde* will also help, especially when accompanied by the angels of the children (interest in every detail of their development) and your own work with those Beings that concern themselves most closely with education. The questions below are nothing of that order, just basic teaching matters, but ones that can easily be overlooked by being taken for granted. They may also be found useful in co-mentoring conversation. As with everything else here – if you don't like the questions, create your own.

1. Have I considered what the class knows already? Am I being too simple or orbiting above their heads?

2. What do I do to ensure the class feels they know where they are going in the lesson? Could I communicate this better?

3. Am I presenting too much (or too little)? Is this what the class needs?

4. Does the class understand what they are learning? (N.B.: if you don't, they won't.)

5. Am I setting appropriate tasks and an appropriate range of tasks?

6. Do I ensure that each individual child hears some positive suggestion, criticism or hint for improvement during the course of a school week? Or am I telling them too many potentially indigestible things?

7. Do I give the class opportunity to reflect on their learning and their differing approaches to the tasks set?

8. Am I providing sufficient opportunities and encouragement for the class to explore what they are learning?

9. Is there anything I could do to increase the confidence of the class in their ability to learn?

10. Anything else that springs to mind and might be relevant?

Take whichever questions seem particularly pertinent. Be clear about the problem. Work out a possible solution. Try it out. Record what happens. Reflect on the result (best with a colleague or two – perfect for co-mentoring). Discuss and prepare to take the next step.

There you have it – action research! If teachers' meetings gave time to discuss of this type of process, they might become the sort of pedagogical heart we like to imagine them to be.

Appendix J:
Care for your voice,
your most precious resource!

Most teachers are professional speakers; in Steiner-Waldorf schools we're concerned with the word, yet very little is said about it and, apart from a little speech formation, most training courses neglect the teacher's voice. Hoarseness, breathing problems, vocal exhaustion and infections of ear, nose and throat are as common among Waldorf teachers as in the teaching profession as a whole. It has been established that teachers are the occupational group with the greatest incidence of voice disorders. Approximately twenty per cent of those attending specialist clinics are likely to be teachers. European studies found that, in any year, fifty per cent of the profession will suffer from poor voice function as a result of illness.[19]

For the Waldorf teacher the voice is one of her or his most important instruments, so much must be carried on the wings of speech. I am also convinced that a great deal of teacher stress not only expresses itself in the voice, but that poor use itself makes it a significant cause of psychological stress.

Here are some suggestions for looking after your voice:

* Consider what F. M. Alexander called your 'use of the self'; your tendency to exert undue pressure on shoulders, back, knees and neck (no wonder the Old Testament prophets criticised the Children of Israel for being 'a stiff-necked people'). When speaking, feel your spine lengthening, keep the eyes forward but not 'blinkered' and relax the knees.

* Imagine that the larynx is relaxed. This can be practised by gently touching the front of the larynx as you speak. You should feel the difference between the more mellow, warmer tone and the more edgy, higher laryngeal production. The latter can easily make for a nervous class. It's always better to lower the voice when you want to get attention than risk the shriek. Similarly, try to avoid sharp vocal attacks. Step back, take in the whole classroom space and go for the foundations. (Remember, very high tones may make people retreat but low ones bring down the building.). Saying, 'Ung-karr-karr, ung-karr-karr, ung-karr-karr' twelve times over morning and evening can also help to increase laryngeal resonance and is especially useful for female teachers, who tend to have the greatest difficulty with this.

* Avoid coughing as much as possible – shouting is also a sort-of vocalised cough and does similar damage (though better one good cough than repeated 'aght' sounds).

* Give as much time as you can to allow your voice (and everyone's nerves) to recover after you have had to make great demands on it. A noisy lesson in the echoing, acoustically-difficult gym hall/eurythmy room/canteen should be followed by a quieter one wherever possible.

* Good ventilation (at home as well as at school) is important.

* Try to avoid dry, dusty rooms – get a humidifier, bring in the goldfish or mop the floor every morning before school starts!

* Avoid foods that dry the vocal tract (at least during the working day) – dairy foods, nuts, chocolate, alcohol and steer clear of the smokers. Fizzy drinks can also cause problems as the gas can force small amounts of stomach acid upwards where they attack the lower edges of the vocal folds. Eating late in the evening can have a similar effect when you lie down to sleep.

* Most importantly; keep well hydrated by drinking plenty of water.

If problems persist, a combination of speech formation and Alexander Technique can be resorted to. I would always advise both unless the speech teacher is very well educated in the physiological aspects as well as the spiritual.

Appendix K:
How are your children sitting?

To find the best chair height, seat children with their knees at 90° and their feet flat on the floor. The distance from the floor to the seating surface shows the chair height you want.

Then find the required worktop height using the tables below:

Chair seat height	13 cm (5 in)	15 cm (6 in)	17 cm (6.5 in)	20 cm (8 in)	25 cm (10 in)	30 cm (12 in)	36 cm (14 in)	41 cm (16 in)	46 cm (18 in)
Table top height	30 cm (12 in)	33 cm (13 in)	36 cm (14 in)	41 cm (16 in)	46 cm (18 in)	51 cm (20 in)	56 cm (22 in)	61–66 cm (24–26 in)	66–76 cm (26–30 in)
Desktop height with allowance for storage compartment	NA	NA	NA	NA	NA	56cm (22 in)	61cm (24 in)	66-71cm (26–28 in)	71-76cm (28–30 in)

Age guide	Size mark	Foot colour code	Chair seat height	Table height
3–4 years	1	Orange	26 cm (10 in)	46 cm (18 in)
4–6 years	2	Violet	31 cm (12 in)	53 cm (21 in)
6–8 years	3	Yellow	35 cm (14 in)	59 cm (23 in)
8–11 years	4	Red	38 cm (15 in)	64 cm (25 in)
11–14 years	5	Green	43 cm (17 in)	71 cm (28 in)
14+	6	Blue	46 cm (18 in)	76 cm (30 in)

The criteria are:

* The chair should allow feet to be placed firmly on the floor (heel and toe).
* The height of the desk should not force the arm upward.
* The chair should be 250 mm (approx.) lower than the desk.
* In practice, no more than two sizes of chairs and usually one of desks will be needed per class.

Appendix L:
An aid to note-taking

Note-taking can be facilitated by the use of standard abbreviations. These are rarely taught (the best way to teach them is, in this case, via imitation). The list overleaf shows, in alphabetical order, some of the most common contractions. Full stops are not used for these for obvious reasons of speed.

I have left these in the handbook because most remain useful. However, given the fact that pupils from Class Six upwards will probably know something about texting, one could well make a start there. The challenge might be to help the pupils understand how the utilitarian simplicity of that type of communication might not support more subtle dialogue.

This could provide a point of entry to the whole subject of the various markers used in writing and their purpose.

> R u redE 2 go out 2nite. I'll sE u b4 8. I'll w8 4 u

It may work for setting up a date, but might be limited when applied to explaining the reasons for Sidney Carton's sacrifice in *A Tale of Two Cities*.

> It +gd th@ I do than hve done b4

Teachers are increasingly likely to have to reckon with how to keep texting in its place (which also means acknowledging where the techniques are appropriate). There is some research to suggest that the use of simplified phonic scripts can bring with them greater difficulties in comprehension. The brief notes in Stockmeyer about shorthand are fascinating, and well worth looking up, when considering how to go about helping the class to take accurate notes.

&	–	and	ctee	–	committee	mech	–	mechanic(al)
etc	–	etcetera	diff	–	difference, different	med	–	medical, medicine
abt	–	about	eg	–	for example	mod	–	modern
afn	–	afternoon (or use am pm – as appropriate)	Eng	–	England, English	MS	–	manuscript
			esp	–	especially	mtg	–	meeting
			ex	–	out of	nb	–	note well
altho	–	although	fr	–	from	neg	–	negative
alw	–	always	gal	–	gallon	pp	–	pages
anon	–	anonymous	gm	–	gramme(s)	prob	–	probably
bn	–	been	ie	–	that is	ref	–	reference
btwn	–	between	info	–	information	secy	–	secretary
cd	–	could	int	–	interest, interesting			
cf	–	compare(d)	lit	–	literally			
cm	–	centimetre(s)	math	–	mathematics			
ctee	–	committee						

Appendix M:
Turning principles into practice

Five, five!

The Steiner Waldorf Schools Fellowship Code of Practice sets out five core organising principles for the whole school:

1. **Respect** for the integrity (unique/spiritual essence) of each individual and of the world in general.

2. **Interest in and positive approach** towards the potential for development in young people in particular and humanity in general.

3. **Recognition** of the central importance of lifelong learning.

4. **Commitment** to the core task of educating children in the light of the above and to encourage, enable.

5. Value the **contribution** of individuals, groups and communities to the improvement of our common heritage.

How might these be translated into classroom practice? We can see these as five core capacities in the daily work of the teacher in the following way:

1. **Respect: Using descriptive affirmation –** saying precisely what you see in the child's behaviour, paying special attention to positive qualities. We try to avoid generalised phrases like, 'Good', or 'Well done', unless we have already said what it is that has been done well. We avoid defining children as 'clever'; that's no more respectful than saying someone is 'stupid'. Putting into more adult words what a child has said is also a mark of respectful pedagogical communication. It is important to encourage our children to express themselves in full sentences. (see point 3 below)

2. **Positive interest: Welcoming mistakes –** if a child gets only right answers, we're *not* doing our job. We learn by mistakes; perfection does not need to learn. It may sound odd to say, 'Thank you for making that mistake', but if you engage with the reasons for the mistake having been made, gratitude is the appropriate response. This leads to...

3. **Learning focus: Providing challenges** – choosing a challenge just outside a child's comfort zone is a matter of pedagogical tact and skill. Some children will be able to reach further than others, but in all cases the key difference between 'a challenge' as something each person raises themselves to from within, and 'stretching' as the deed of an educational Procrustes, is absolute we need to involve the former, not the latter for healthy learning.

4. **Developing commitment: Providing time for practice** – acquiring skills involves repetition. Handwriting, spelling, basic number facts, grammar all need plenty of practice. Education also involves training. Practice can be enlivened, or reinvigorated if a small extra (meaningful) challenge is added.

5. **Enabling contribution: Encouraging independence** – avoid over teaching, step back and observe. Not everything can, or should flow from the teacher. This is also a practical form of respect. Expect and encourage self-reliance as this will breed self-confidence.

Further Reading

The following is not a comprehensive listing of Waldorf or other educational source material, simply a selection of some of the essentials and lesser-known background reading. I have not included Rudolf Steiner's lectures here, nor any general books, such as the *Way of the Child*. The emphasis here is on books for the class teacher, whether from Waldorf or other sources, that the reader may find practically useful.

Allen, Jon, *Drawing Geometry*, Floris Books, 2007

Anderson, Henning, Archie Duncanson and Verner Pedersen, *Active Arithmetic: Movement and mathematics teaching in the lower grades of a Waldorf school*, Waldorf Publications 2014

Bain, George, *Celtic Art: the Methods of Construction*, Constable 1996

Barnes, Henry, ed., *Towards a Deepening of Waldorf Education*, Pedagogical Section of the School of Spiritual Science 1991

Berry, Cicely, *Voice and the Actor*, Jossey Bass 1991

Brooking-Payne, Kim, *Games Children Play*, Hawthorn Press 1997

Cornell, Joseph, *Sharing Nature with Children*, Dawn Publications 1999

Davidson, Norman, *Sky Phenomena: A Guide to naked-eye observation of the stars*, Lindisfarne Books 2001

Diggins, Julia E., *String, Straight-edge and Shadow: The Story of Geometry*, Floris Books 2018

Evans, Michael and Iain Rodger, *Healing for Body, Soul and Spirit*, Floris Books 2000

Franceschelli, Amos, *Algebra:Mathematics for grades 6, 7 and 8*, Mercury Press 1995

— *Mensuration*, Mercury Press 2000

Grohmann, Gerbert, *The Living World of the Plants: A Book for children and students of nature*, Waldorf Publications 1999

Hahn, Herbert, *From the Wellsprings of the Soul: Towards the religious teaching of the young*, Steiner Schools Fellowship 1977

van Haren, Wil and Rudolf Kischnick, *Child's Play: Games for children and teenagers, vol. 1 & 2*, Hawthorn Press 1996

Harrer, Dorothy, *An English Manual*, Waldorf Publications 2004

— *Math Lessons for Elementary Grades*, Waldorf Publications 2005

— *Chapters from Ancient History*, Waldorf Publications 2016

Goddard, Sally, *Reflexes Learning and Behaviour*, Fern Ridge Press 2015

Jacobs, Rita, *Music for Young Children*, Hawthorn Press 1991

Jaffke, Freya, *Work and Play in Early Childhood*, Floris Books 1996

— *Celebrations Festivals with Children*, Floris Books 2011

Jarman, Ron, *Teaching Mathematics in Rudolf Steiner Schools for Classes I–VIII*, Hawthorn Press 2000

Jünemann, Margrit and Fritz Weimann, *Drawing and Painting in Rudolf Steiner Schools*, Hawthorn Press 1994

Klocek, Dennis, *Drawing from the Book of Nature*, Rudolf Steiner College Press 2000

Knierim, Julius, *Quintenlieder*, Freies Geistesleben 1994

Koepke, Hermann, *Encountering the Self: Transformation and destiny in the ninth year*, Steiner Books 1999

— see also the series that includes *Animals: An Imaginative Zoology*, Floris Books 2013

Kovacs, Charles, lesson notes and various resource books, most available from Floris Books

Kutzli, Rudolph, *Creative Form Drawing: Workbook One*, Hawthorn Press 2007

von Mackensen, Manfred, *A Phenomena-Based Physics, vol. 1–3*, Waldorf Publications 1994

McAllen, Audrey E., *The Listening Ear: The development of speech as an influence in early education*, Hawthorn Press 1990

Martin, Michael, ed., *Arts and Crafts in Waldorf Schools: An integrated approach to craft work in Steiner Waldorf schools*, Floris Books 2017

Masters, Brien, *A Waldorf Song Book*, Floris Books 2015

Matthews, Paul, *Sing Me the Creation*, Hawthorn Press 2015

Mees, L.F.C., *Secrets of the Skeleton: Form in Metamorphosis*, SteinerBooks Inc. 1985

Mellon, Nancy, *Storytelling and the Art of Imagination*, Yellow Moon Press 2003

— *Storytelling with Children*, Hawthorne Press 2013

Meyer, Rudolf, *The Wisdom of Fairy Tales*, Floris Books 1995

Müller, Heinz, *Report Verses in Rudolf Steiner's Art of Education*, Floris Books 2013

Nash-Wortham, Mary and Jean Hunt, *Take Time*, 5th edition, Robinswood Press 2008

Pittis, Arthur, *Pedagogical Theatre: Dramaturgy and performance practice for the lower and middle school grades*, Waldorf Publications 2016

Rawson, Martin and Kevin Avison, eds., *Towards Creative Teaching: Notes to an Evolving Curriculum for Steiner Waldorf Class Teachers*, Floris Books 2013

Rawson, Martyn and Michael Rose, *Ready to Learn: From birth to school readiness*, Hawthorn Press 2006

Rawson, Martin, Kevin Avison and Tobias Richter, eds., *The Tasks and Content of the Steiner-Waldorf Curriculum*, Floris Books 2014

Renwick Sheen, A., *Geometry and the Imagination: The imaginative treatment of geometry in Waldorf education*, Waldorf Publications 2002

Schwartz, Eugene, *Why the Setting Sun Turns Red: And other pedagogical stories*, Waldorf Publications 2004

Smyth, Nell, *Drama at the Heart: Teaching Drama in Steiner-Waldorf Schools*, Floris Books 2016

Squires, Geoffrey, *Trouble-Shooting Your Teaching: A step-by-step guide to analysing and improving your practice*, Routledge 2002

Staley, Betty K., *Hear the Voice of the Griot! A guide to African geography, history and culture*, Rudolf Steiner College Press 1997

Stockmeyer, E. A. Karl, *Rudolf Steiner's Curriculum for Waldorf Schools*, Floris Books 2015

Streit, Jakob, *And There was Light*, Waldorf Publications 2007

— *What Animals Say to Each Other*, Waldorf Publications 2014

— *Journey to the Promised Land*, Waldorf Publications 2015

Stribley, Miriam, *The Calligraphy Source Book*, Running Press 1986

Swann, Michael, *Practical English Usage*, Oxford University Press 2005

Taylor, Micheal, *Fingers Strings: A Book of Cat's Cradles and String Figures*, Floris Books 2008

Thaulow, Henrik, *Living Lines*, Floris Books 2019

Thody, Angela, Barbara Gray and Derek Bowden, *The Teacher's Survival Guide*, Network Continuum Education 2007

Thomas, Heather, *A Journey Through Time in Verse and Rhyme*, Floris Books 1998

Trostli, Roberto, *Physics is Fun: A sourcebook for teachers*, Waldorf Publications 1995

Ulin, Bengt, *Finding the Path: Themes and methods for the teaching of mathematics in a Waldorf school*, Waldorf Publications 1996

— *Child's Play 3: Games for life for children & teenagers*, Hawthorn Press 1994

Walker, Lester, *Housebuilding for Children: Step-by-step guides for houses children can build themselves*, Overlook Press 2007

Weston, M., *Festivals Together: A guide to multi-cultural celebration*, Hawthorn Press 1993

Wildgruber, Thomas. *Painting and Drawing in Waldorf Schools: Classes 1 to 8*, Floris Books 2012

Wilkinson, Roy, *Origin and Development of Language*, Hawthorn Press 1998

— see also Wilkinson's other publications on a variety of subjects

York, Jamie, *A Student's Workbook for Mathematics*, (available for Classes Six to Eight), Floris Books 2016

— *A Teacher's Source Book for Mathematics in Classes 6 to 8*, Floris Books 2016

York, Jamie, Randy Evans and Mick Follari, *Fun with Maths Puzzles, Games and More*, Floris Books 2019

York, Jamie, Nettie Fabrie and Wim Gottenbos, *A Teacher's Source Book for Mathematics in Classes 1 to 5*, Floris Books 2017

Endnotes

1. A version of those values is set out in the preamble to the SWSF Code of Practice

2. See Barfield, O, *Romanticism Comes of Age* and *The Rediscovery of Meaning*

3. Stockmeyer, E.A.K, *Rudolf Steiner's Curriculum*, Floris Books, 2015

4. Floris Books edition, 2014

5. Steiner, R, *Human Values in Education*, Arnheim, 21st August 1924

6. See Checklist for details!

7. In *Foundations of Human Experience / Study of Man*, the closing word form the motto: 'Imbue thyself with the power of imagination; Have courage for the truth; Sharpen thy feeling for responsibility of soul'

8. Wiseacres may have had the original from Saint Bernard of Clairvaux: 'L'enfer est plein de bonnes volontés ou désirs'

9. It is often impossible to arrange things to allow for four-week Morning Lessons in all cases. Where this can be arranged, it will be found, for many subjects, that this allows sufficient time for a real immersion in and exploration of a topic. 28 days works with natural (life rhythms) in a way that shorter periods do not.

10. 'Achieved' should only be used when the child has demonstrated a secure use of the skill in varied contexts. Evidence of achievement should always be available.

11. **Subordinate Clauses** contain subject and a verb whose tense follows that of the main verb. For example, 'This is the book that will answer your questions'.
    Relative Clauses serve to distinguish the noun they follow from other nouns of the same class. 'The man who told us this wishes to remain anonymous.'
    Conditional Clauses are usually signalled by the word 'if', or alternatively by 'unless', 'but for', 'provided', 'suppose' or 'otherwise'. 'If I were you, I would read this handbook. You will be late unless you start now.'
    Clauses of Comparison are related to the use of simile. 'Asking for help from him is like feeding canapés to a gannet.' or 'It is better to say too little than to say too much'.
    Clauses of Concession are introduced by 'though', 'although', 'even if', 'no matter', 'however', 'plus' adjective/adverb and sometimes 'whatever'. For example, 'However hard you work, it will never be hard enough'.
    Nouns in apposition The Steiner Schools Fellowship, an association of Waldorf Schools in Britain, does what it can.

12. The teacher must be a person of initiative in everything that they do, great and small. The teacher should be one who is interested in the being of the whole world and of humanity. The teacher must be one who never makes a compromise with what is untrue. The teacher must never get stale or grow sour.

13. See *Games Children Play: How Games and Sport Help Children Develop* by Kim Brooking-Payne (Hawthorn Press, 1996).

14. Form-drawing skills can be practised usefully in association with other Morning Lessons (e.g., forms connected with number, preparation for writing) and as extra lessons.

15. Although emphasis is placed upon the archetypal activity, it is important not to overlook the need to bring these things up to date, thus connecting them with the children's everyday experience. For

More books for Steiner-Waldorf teachers

Without being restrictive or prescriptive, this wonderful book provides helpful suggestions to both class teachers and subject specialists, adding to the richness and imagination of each teacher's own work.

A truly comprehensive overview of all main-lesson and accompanying subjects, this book offers a wealth of guidance, knowledge and inspiration for Waldorf class teachers on planning, shaping and developing lessons for Classes 1 to 8.

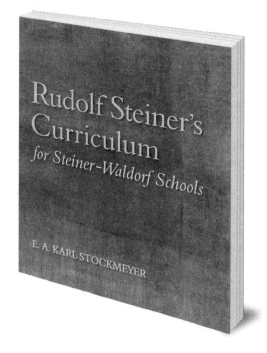

This important book for all Steiner-Waldorf teachers gets to the heart of Steiner's ideas on education and child development with an in-depth exploration of the curriculum of the first Waldorf school, expanding on the original 'Lehrplan'.

Divided into sections, the book outlines Steiner's comments on schools and lessons in general, as well as many details on his thinking on specific issues ranging from different age groups to classroom decoration and arrangement.

florisbooks.co.uk

The
Tasks *and*
Content
of the Steiner-Waldorf Curriculum

Edited by
KEVIN AVISON *and*
MARTYN RAWSON

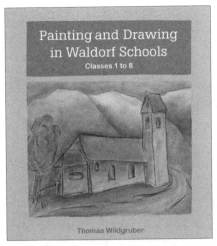

Painting and Drawing
in Waldorf Schools
Classes 1 to 8

Thomas Wildgruber

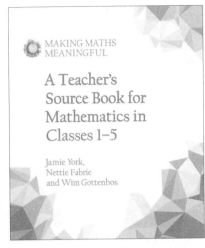

MAKING MATHS
MEANINGFUL

A Teacher's
Source Book for
Mathematics in
Classes 1–5

Jamie York,
Nettie Fabrie
and Wim Gottenbos

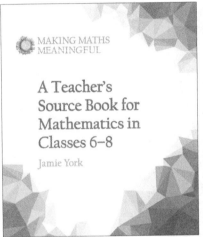

MAKING MATHS
MEANINGFUL

A Teacher's
Source Book for
Mathematics in
Classes 6–8

Jamie York

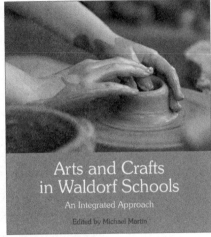

Arts and Crafts
in Waldorf Schools
An Integrated Approach
Edited by Michael Martin

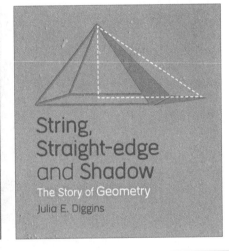

String,
Straight-edge
and Shadow
The Story of Geometry
Julia E. Diggins

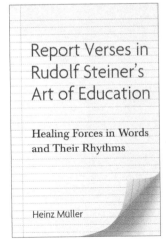

Report Verses in
Rudolf Steiner's
Art of Education

Healing Forces in Words
and Their Rhythms

Heinz Müller

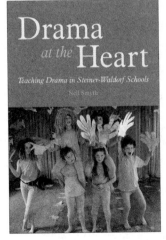

Drama
at the Heart
Teaching Drama in Steiner-Waldorf Schools
Nell Smyth

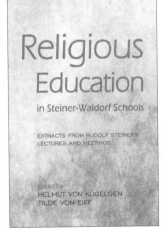

Religious
Education
in Steiner-Waldorf Schools

EXTRACTS FROM RUDOLF STEINER'S
LECTURES AND MEETINGS

Edited by
HELMUT VON KÜGELGEN
TILDE VON EIFF

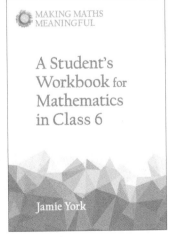

MAKING MATHS
MEANINGFUL

A Student's
Workbook for
Mathematics
in Class 6

Jamie York

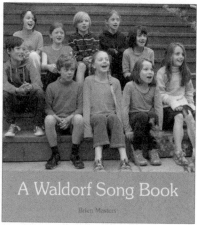

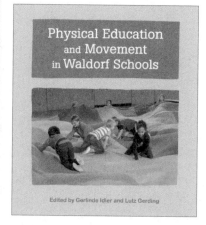

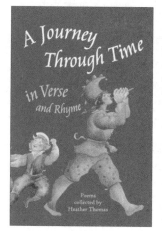

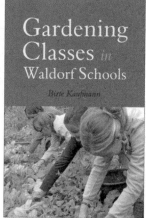

Floris Books